Donald
Keeling

Bought on Market stall

THE PLEASURES OF
PARIS

The Pleasures Of
PARIS

Michael Bond

PAVILION
MICHAEL JOSEPH

First published in Great Britain in 1987 by
Pavilion Books Ltd, 196 Shaftesbury Avenue,
London WC2H 8JL
in association with Michael Joseph Ltd,
27 Wrights Lane, W8 5TZ

Designed by Nick Hand

Film processing Leith Air Ltd
Cameras Leica R4 and Contax 137
Film FP4 and XP1
Map references courtesy of Michelin from Michelin
Plan de Paris No. 10

British Library Cataloguing in Publication Data
        Bond, Michael
            The pleasures of Paris.
            1. Restaurants, lunch rooms, etc. ——
            France —— Paris
            I. Title
            647'.9544'36   TX910.F8
            ISBN 1-85145-107-2

Typeset in Monophoto Bodoni 504
by MS Filmsetting Limited, Frome, Somerset
Printed and bound in Great Britain by Butler and Tanner Ltd

CONTENTS

*The newspapers have given the
rage of going to Paris a good name;
they call it the French disease.*

Horace Walpole, 1717–1797

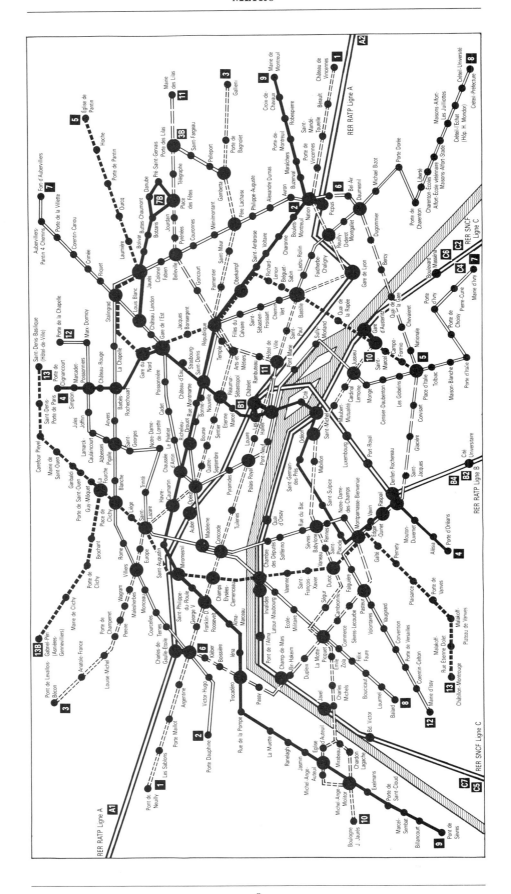

INTRODUCTION

My first visit to France took place one cold, but sunny winter's day in 1945. I stepped off the gang-plank of a cross-channel troopship and suddenly, after what was, after all, a comparatively short journey, found myself in a totally different world. The people were different, the architecture was different, the language was different, and the food was certainly different. Even the very air had a totally different smell to it.

It was a case of love at first sight, and unlike some other love affairs in my life, it has stood the test of time for over forty years and shows no sign of waning.

My regiment was *en route* to the Middle East and the journey by train was taken at a snail's pace. There wasn't much left of the French railways and we were constantly being diverted, so I had plenty of time to absorb my new surroundings; from the flat, shell-shocked plains of the north, round Paris and down the Rhône Valley, to the relative warmth and the red-tiled roofs of the south, and I knew that I would return as soon as I could, for I felt strangely happy.

After the war was over I took a holiday in Brittany, and some years later honeymooned there. We stayed at a small hotel in St Briac, and it was there that I encountered my first artichoke. Arriving down to dinner before anyone else, and never having seen one, we ate it all, down to the very last leaf; no mean feat, and one which not only took an inordinately long time, but caused the chef to peer round the kitchen door at one point and gaze at us as if he could hardly believe his eyes, which he probably couldn't, poor man. It must have confirmed his worst suspicions about the British, as indeed it did for some of the other residents about the French, as they trooped into the dining-room and attempted to follow our example.

Honour was restored after several more courses when I threw caution to the wind and rather grandly ordered a *soufflé Grand Marnier* – a speciality of the restaurant, which in those days had a star in the *Michelin Guide*. It was and remains the biggest soufflé I have ever seen, carried into the restaurant by the chef himself, perhaps as a kind of prize, and the other guests gathered round to watch us eat it.

We spent an unhappy night sitting up in bed clutching our stomachs, and given the fact that over the years I have several times managed to block our waste disposal machine by feeding it with artichoke leaves, I can understand why. Our own waste disposals were blocked for many days afterwards. But my love for France remained untarnished. In my eyes, it could do no wrong.

Since those days I have been back as often as possible, travelling the length and breadth of the country, either on holiday, or for a time when I was working on television scripts, making an annual pilgrimage to the Cannes Television Festival, along with a gourmet friend, who was also, let it be said, a gourmand; he, armed with the *Michelin Guide*, seeking out hotels boasting a red rocking chair and issuing ETA's, while I did the driving. Some of our journeys were very circuitous indeed, as you can imagine.

In recent years, having embarked on a series of novels about a French detective turned food inspector, and his faithful hound cum food taster, Pommes Frites, I've managed to combine work with pleasure in the nicest possible way as I go in search of new locations and background material.

Somewhere along the line I acquired a small flat in Paris. It came about late one evening when I was sitting drinking with a French friend discussing the things one regretted never having done. I happened to say that I wished I could have lived in Paris for a small part of my life. He suddenly sobered up and announced that his daughter had a flat in Montmartre she wished to dispose of. Several weeks later it was mine and I can still hardly believe my good fortune. Each time I go there it is with a feeling of mounting excitement. Somewhere, halfway across the Channel, life seems to begin.

And that, I suppose, is the secret about the French, that feeling for life and the way it should be lived. There are those who say that France would be wonderful if it wasn't for the French, but that, of course, is nonsense. France is the way it is because of the French. They can, on occasion, be unbelievably rude, for they never do things by halves, but I think it would be true to say that on the whole I have met more genuine kindness and politeness there than I have any-where else, and even in the big cities they still take time to observe the small niceties and courtesies of life. Above all, they care, and they have a pride in doing things correctly and a sense of style even if it only involves serving a cup of coffee. They also have an inbuilt sense of priorities which is peculiarly their own.

Two things illustrate what I mean. One evening recently I was sitting in a small restaurant in Paris (*Aux Petits Pères* for those who read on), when two friends of the owner came in, bringing with them a large dog. Kisses were duly exchanged and the waitresses came forward to shake hands. Then came the first quesion, uttered with great seriousness and concern. Not 'Would you care for an *apéritif*?' or 'Where would you like to sit?', but 'Has he eaten?' They were referring to the dog. It wouldn't happen anywhere else. Pommes Frites would have approved.

The other story is told by Rudolph Chelminski in his excellent and eminently readable book *The French at Table*. It concerns a certain Père Baroillet, priest to the Troisgros family, owners of the famous three-star restaurant in Roanne, a dedicated gourmet and connoisseur of wine, who before the war had been *curé* of Meursault.

When the brothers Jean and Pierre Troisgros were attending a private commemorative service for their father following his death, it fell to Père Baroillet to take the mass. Following the approved routine, as he had done many hundreds of times before for other departed souls, he came to the moment of Consecration, and as he tenderly cradled the chalice of wine in his hands he turned to speak to the brothers and ad libbed a little piece of information which he was sure would interest them.

'*C'est un petit aligoté de chez Colin,*' he announced before tasting it and getting on with his work.

Again, it could only happen in France.

This book began as a labour of love – a very small list of restaurants for use by anyone who happened to be staying in the apartment. But like Topsy it somehow just grew and grew. It took me to parts of Paris I wouldn't otherwise have visited and to restaurants I might never have known about. It also gave me an opportunity to indulge another love – photography – and to justify a compulsion for buying new equipment which might never have been used.

It remained a labour of love, which is really how all books should be written. The fact that it is being published is an added bonus, for it is nice to be able to share the pleasures of life, and the pleasures of Paris are boundless.

This is a book for those who like exploring big cities and who also enjoy eating. Happily, Paris caters well for both pursuits. It is beautiful and manageable and cafés and restaurants abound.

The whole is bounded by the *Périphérique*, a giant circular road built on the site of what was once the city fortifications and a means of collecting taxes from anyone who wished to enter. Within the *Périphérique* Paris is divided into twenty *arrondissements*, each of which is sub-divided again into *quartiers*.

Like most things French, it is very logical. If you stand on one of the thirty-three bridges spanning the river Seine and face the way the

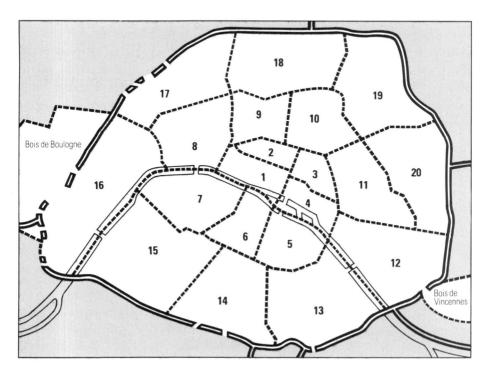

Paris is divided into twenty arrondissements

current is flowing, the right bank is on your right and the left bank is on your left. Streets which run perpendicular to the river Seine have numbers beginning at the end nearest the river. Streets which run parallel to the Seine have numbers which run from east to west. You can't get much more logical than that.

Because each arrondissement tends to have its own particular and unique character, that is the way this book has been divided up, with suggestions for places to visit, things to do and places in which to eat. Lighted street maps abound, but a pocket edition of the *Plan Guide Blay* by arrondissement and a *Michelin Green Guide* will be invaluable.

GETTING ABOUT

Taxis don't cruise around looking for fares as in other cities – one light on the roof means they are occupied, two they are free, none, they are going home! – so restaurants are related to the nearest Metro station. The Metro is efficient and the trains are regular – every ninety seconds in the rush hour. Few stations are more than five hundred metres apart, although when you are changing lines (look for the CORRESPONDANCE sign) it may feel like it, for at some stations the corridors can seem endless. This is because the lines are rarely more than a few metres below the surface and when the Metro was built it followed the middle of the *boulevards* in order to avoid damage to the buildings on either side and possible expensive insurance claims. It also accounts for the somewhat tortuous route it often follows. The maps show exactly where you are below ground at any given point.

A flat-rate ticket will take you anywhere you like and *carnets* of ten can be bought cheaply at any Metro station. Paris Sesame tickets valid for periods of two, four or seven days are available from certain stations on production of a passport and these can also be used on the buses. Tickets are validated when you pass through the automatic barriers, but don't throw them away or make them into aeroplanes as terrifying and humourless ladies hunt in pairs and will fine you on the spot if you don't produce one.

Buses are more fun and at night often quicker, but unless you have a Sesame ticket they are slightly more expensive; two ordinary tickets are sometimes needed to complete a journey and it is as well to study the route map at each stop before you board in order to find out how many 'sections' you will be using. Once on board you will need to validate your ticket(s) in a machine alongside the driver. You will also discover that everyone else will have some kind of pass – either because they are young or old, infirm, pregnant or were wounded in one of the wars.

The latest aids to getting about, now being installed in selected Metro stations and other points around the city, are computerized SITU machines. You simply type in the name of the street you are going to and by what means you wish to travel – by Metro, bus or on foot – and you receive a print-out showing the quickest route.

EATING OUT

Despite inflation, Paris abounds in cheap restaurants – something like ten thousand at the last count – where you can be assured of a satisfying meal at a reasonable price, including wine and service. The menu will be displayed outside, and if the inside is full of French people tucking in, then you will be on safe ground.

There is no word in the French language for 'home' as we know it. Home to a Frenchman tends to include the surrounding eating establishments and they do make much more use of them than we do, so they like to get value for money. The local *bistro* is where they meet, engage in conversation, leave messages, make telephone calls, eat, drink, and sometimes sleep it off afterwards.

More often than not the owners are treated like heads of the family, hence the widespread use of the prefixes 'Mère' and 'Père' in their names.

The restaurants in this book are mainly middle-of-the-road, with a sprinkling of bistros thrown in. The temples of gastronomy, with one exception, have been excluded; they are in all the guides anyway, and the choice is yours.

On the basis that in life you tend to get what you pay for, all of them give good value for money. A lot will depend on your taste in wine. If you like to indulge yourself before, during and after a meal you will pay for it accordingly. In any case prices tend to go up rather than down, so it is as well to consult the latest *Michelin* or *Gault-Millau* guide before booking; and book you must at most of those listed.

French cooking has changed a good deal over the past few years. There is nothing really new about *nouvelle cuisine*, which is a journalistic phrase anyway, but if it has done nothing else, with its emphasis on lightness and colour, it has underlined the need for fresh ingredients. Stale ingredients can no longer be disguised by the use of heavy sauces. If there is any one factor above all which raises French cooking above that of other nations it is the quality of the ingredients. If a demand is created a market will exist, and French chefs demand and get fresh produce.

Now that things have settled down again there is a growing tendency to combine the best of the old with that of the new, and the result is probably better and healthier for us all in the long run, but if you hanker, as I often do, for a good, hearty old-fashioned meal, then look at the outside of the restaurant first, study the menu, and then peer through the lace curtains at the people inside. The first will most likely be dark brown in colour, the second either typed or hand-written, and the occupants will be hard at work, concentrating on the job in hand. None of them will have seen a slice of kiwi fruit in years.

1er ARRONDISSEMENT

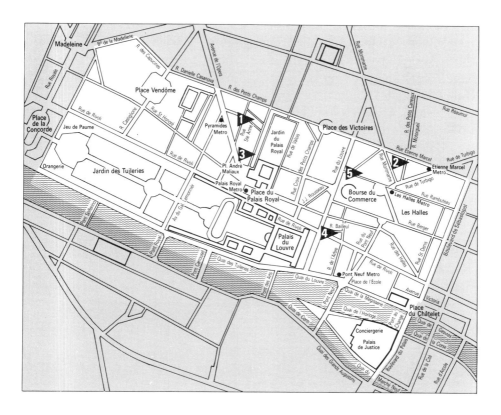

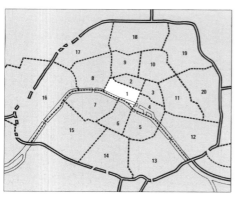

1. Chez Pauline
2. Escargot Montorgueil
3. Pierre Traiteur
4. Chez la Vieille
5. Au Pied de Cochon

Paris is the sum of many things; the grey of its rooftops, the colour of its stone, the wrought-iron chairs dotted about the parks and squares, its *Grands Boulevards*, the constant joy of discovering something new down little alley-ways and *passages*, followed by the glimpse of a familiar landmark in the distance, the pavement cafés, its sense of being 'lived-in', its elegance and style living in perfect harmony alongside the very worst in chrome and plate, the feeling of life and vibrance in the air, and perhaps above all the overwhelming sense of history which permeates everything.

Nowhere is this more in evidence than on the boat-shaped Ile de la Cité, the prow of which is seen overleaf from the roof terrace of the great department store La Samaritaine, itself something of an historical monument, and as good a place as any to get one's bearings over a cup of coffee before setting out on a voyage of exploration.

If the stone walls and buttresses of Paris's oldest bridge, the Pont Neuf, have an unaccustomed sheen to them it is because they have been specially gift-wrapped for the occasion by 'Christo', a Bulgarian 'packaging artist' who began his unusual occupation in a small way during the sixties parcelling up trees and oil drums, and worked his way up to fulfil a ten-year-old ambition in Paris.

The Ile de la Cité is where it all began in the year 250 BC. First the Parisii came from Gaul and set up camp there. Then in 53 BC it

was the turn of the Romans, who called it Lutetia — meaning 'habitation surrounded by water'. Under the Romans it prospered and its boat shape became a symbol of the fishermen. In AD 250 Christianity arrived in the form of St Denis, who became the city's first bishop, and in AD 360 its name was officially changed to Paris and the fishermen's symbol became that of Paris itself, along with the motto 'fluctuat nec murgitur' — 'she is tossed but does not sink'.

Paris's oldest bridge, the Pont Neuf, seen from the rooftop café of that haven of nostalgia, the Samaritan department store.

There have always been fishermen on the banks of the Ile de la Cité, and in Paris fishermen never lack hangers-on and watchers and advisers, for the French like nothing better than to air their opinions and to get themselves involved in a discussion. Give them a simple matter like baiting a hook and they can complicate it in a matter of moments. It's what life is all about.

The western half of the Ile de la Cité, which constitutes the bottom right-hand corner of the 1st arrondissement, is dominated by La Conciergerie, that most sinister of French prisons with its memories of post-Revolutionary horrors when over 2,600 prisoners met their death, and Marie Antoinette, Madame du Barry, Danton and Robespierre were among those who took it in turn to join the queue to have their hair shorn before making the journey by tumbril to the Place de la Concorde. It was part of the original Royal Palace, which paradoxically contains that masterpiece of thirteenth-century French architecture, the church of Sainte-Chapelle, with its fifteen hundred square yards of stained glass windows contained within incredibly slender pillars and buttresses.

Behind the Conciergerie, where Paris's oldest bridge, the Pont Neuf, crosses the island, are some steps which lead down to the little pointed Square de Vert Galant, a good place for a picnic if you don't mind sharing it with young lovers trying to emulate Henri IV's reputation for amorous enterprise which gave the square its name.

On the right bank of the Seine is the Quai de la Mégisserie, once, as its name suggests, ripe with the smell of leather tanning, now noisy with rows of pet-shops intermingling with garden centres.

Further along is the Louvre, where you can either spend the rest of your time in Paris (except Tuesdays), or else emulate Art Buchwald's Mr Stone who, in 1955, clipped two seconds off the previous record of doing the six-minute tour, taking in its three most important exhibits, 'The Winged Victory of Samothrace', 'Venus de Milo' and the 'Mona Lisa'.

The Louvre, at present in the throes of a vast rebuilding programme, marks the beginning of the Tuileries: once a site for digging clay for tile-making – hence its name. There are pony rides and cafés, statuary galore, and plenty of chairs for sitting on, although if you are male and alone beware of doing it on the Seine side of the park, especially in the late afternoon, and especially anywhere near the underground passage for piétons; you won't be alone for long! At the Place de la Concorde end of the gardens there is a large round pond whose seemingly placid waters become alive with carp the moment you drop a piece of bread in. On summer weekdays children sail their toy boats there and on Sunday mornings flocks of dedicated model boat owners descend on it, fiddling with their radio controls or trying to get their miniature engines to start. Like the fishermen on the Ile de la Cité, they are never short of an audience or helpful advice.

Despite its long arcaded walk, the Rue de Rivoli, which runs along the opposite side of the Tuileries to the Seine, is a disappointment: crowded with tourists and a hotch-potch of shops catering for their needs; but at No. 248 there is a branch of W. H. Smith, where you can buy English books and newspapers and if you so wish take them upstairs to read over a cup of tea or a snack lunch.

Across the Rue de Rivoli, back in the Tuileries, is the Jeu de Paume. Its magnificent collection of Impressionist paintings has been transferred to the Museum of the Nineteenth Century on the other side of the Seine, and it now houses temporary exhibitions. In the opposite corner of the gardens is the Orangerie, home of Monet's giant circular painting and the crowning masterpiece of his career, the Waterlilies at Giverny.

The French have an ambivalent attitude towards animals and birds. On the whole, short of having the vote, dogs fare better in Paris than in most capital cities, perhaps because there are over 700,000 of them. They are allowed into restaurants and, provided their owners can afford to foot the bill, they can order what they like. Afterwards, they have white silhouettes painted on the side of the *trottoir* for their convenience, and if they don't make it in time, uniformed men on Yamaha motor cycles, members of *Trottoir Net*, follow on behind and clear up after them.

On the other hand, give a Frenchman something that moves, be it on the ocean bed or on land, and he will happily eat it. It's hard to tell if the old lady sitting in the gardens of the Palais-Royal pictured on the next page is simply sharing her lunch or whether she has her eye on a likely candidate for the evening meal.

Nowadays the Palais-Royal presents a very orderly face to the world. Long lines of identical windows on either side of the gardens look down on to rows of identical trees, which in turn reflect the symmetry of the rose beds, the paths, and the fountain in the centre. Old ladies do their knitting, while younger ones watch over their children playing in the sand pits at the far end.

But it wasn't always so. The history of the Palais-Royal is a

stormy one, more revolutionary at times than royal. It was at No. 177 that Charlotte Corday bought the dagger she used to murder Marat in his bath, and it was here on Sunday, 12 July 1789 that Camille Desmoulins made his famous speech which two days later resulted in the storming of the Bastille. The Palais-Royal flourished as a centre of vice and iniquity for many years after the Revolution. Gambling houses and brothels filled the arcades, untouched by the police, who were barred entry. Gradually, however, order was restored and its last great drama came in 1871 when it was set on fire by the Communards and largely destroyed. In recent years Jean Cocteau lived here and Colette spent her last years at 9 Rue de Beaujolais, dining at the Palais-Royal's most famous restaurant, *Le Grand Vefour*.

It was in this area that the word 'restaurant' was first coined by its owner, the aptly named Monsieur Boulanger, who unwittingly became a trend-setter at a time when many chefs to the wealthy suddenly found themselves out of work following the Revolution.

That guardian of the French spoken word, the state-subsidized Comédie Française, stands alongside the Palais-Royal in the Place André Malraux, who was a one-time resident. Known for their impeccable diction and ability to play passionate love scenes while standing on opposite sides of the stage, the actors, some of whom spend their entire working lives with the company, enjoy the rare privilege, under a ruling dated 1860, of sharing in the box office receipts according to seniority. On display upstairs is the chair in which Molière collapsed on stage while appearing in his own play Le Malade Imaginaire in 1673.

There are no theatrical neon signs to be seen in the Place Vendôme after dark, only the discreet lighting emanating from the Ritz Hotel, some very prestigious and expensive jewellers, merchant banks, the Ministry of Justice and the British Tourist Authority. None of them, except possibly the BTA, need to advertise their presence; those who know about these things will find their way there anyway.

Classically severe, elegant, wealthy, aloof, symmetrical, vast; the Place Vendôme is all of these things. In the beginning it was a mere façade in limestone, and even when buildings were added at the rear the only way in was through the back. Chopin died at No. 12. Dr Mesmer, founder of Mesmerism, held sessions at No. 16 when he lived there, and Chanel spent the last years of her life at the Ritz.

In the middle of it all is the statue of Napoleon dressed in his Caesar outfit, as he was in the beginning. Henri IV occupied the position while Napoleon was out of favour, then the Emperor reappeared in military uniform, only to lose his perch once again when the column was pulled down at the time of the Commune. Gustave Courbet, the artist, who was suspected of being behind the plot, was made to repair it at his own expense.

Dividing the 1st arrondissement neatly into north and south is the Rue St Honoré, that chicest of shopping streets. Going west it leads on to even better things in the 8th when it becomes the Rue du Faubourg St Honoré; going east it leads to Les Halles.

Holes have always been an endless source of fascination, on a par with sand and water. Dig a hole in the ground, then erect a fence around it and you will be assured of an endless stream of people doing their level best to see what's going on inside.

When the old market at Les Halles was uprooted and transferred to Rungis, it left a mammoth hole right in the centre of Paris. Arguments raged for many years on what to do with it. Some wanted to fill it in, thus creating a series of smaller holes elsewhere. President Pompidou wanted to build a huge trade and business centre. Giscard d'Estaing opted for giving it back to the Parisians on a grand scale, and so Le Forum des Halles was born. The scale is certainly grand. In the hole itself there are descending levels of over two hundred shops, ten cinemas, restaurants, car parks, and a Metro station. Above ground the fifty-four acre site is a vast conglomeration in concrete, glass and steel, of offices and apartments, fountains, landscaped gardens, pools and a marvellous children's adventure playground.

You may like it, or you may hate it, but it's hard to ignore it completely, and there is too much concrete for it ever to go away. Perhaps more than anywhere else in Paris it reflects the way the French have embraced the latter half of the twentieth century. Baron Haussman would have been very jealous.

The Forum des Halles.

5 Rue Villedo
Tel: 42.96.20.70
Cards: CB, VISA
Closed: Saturday
evening, Sunday
Nearest Metro:
Pyramides (7)
Map ref: 1

Chez Pauline is a happy restaurant. The owners are happy, the staff are happy, the customers are happy; consequently eating there is a happy experience, for even the food seems affected.

It was well known as a bistro before the war, when Curnonsky, the King of Gourmets, used to eat there regularly (his corner seat is marked by a plaque), and was taken over by Monsieur and Madame Paul Génin in the early fifties. Nowadays the son, André, is in charge, but the cooking remains as good as ever – a blend of classical Burgundian with 'nouvelle' overtones in keeping with the times.

Specialities handed down over the years are: Morvan ham *en croûte*, truffled Bresse chicken, *ris de veau en croûte, boeuf Bourguignon* and many others, but if you want to sample as many as possible without feeling overwhelmed, then the *menu dégustation* can be strongly recommended; the portions are exactly right. If you choose to eat *à la carte*, there is a fixed routine for daily specialities and it will allow you to end up with their famous *gâteau de riz*. As might be expected, the wine list is high on wines from Burgundy, and there is a good selection of Beaujolais.

The restaurant is on two floors. Downstairs is where all the action is; upstairs is quieter and more spread out. Monsieur Génin often lectures in the USA, and during the tourist season many of his pupils return the compliment by eating *Chez Pauline*.

The motto in the restaurant is a quote from Winston Churchill – 'There is nothing wrong with change, as long as it is in the right direction; to be perfect is to have changed often'. One wouldn't wish *Chez Pauline* to change, it seems exactly right as it is.

38 Rue Montorgueil
Tel: 42.36.83.51
Cards: AE, DC, EC, VISA
Closed: Monday, Tuesday, two weeks in August
Nearest Metro: Etienne Marcel (4)
Map ref: 2

This restaurant has an entry in *Gault-Millau* which devotes almost as much space to the décor as it does to the food, and no entry at all in *Michelin*. Given the former's devotion to *nouvelle cuisine*, which is not what the *Escargot Montorgueil* is all about, it says a lot for the décor, with its genuine Second Empire ceilings, dark panelling, wall mirrors and chandeliers.

As the name suggests, snails are a speciality; they even appear in graphic form on the serviettes. Only in France would they think of adding to the exquisite décor with a giant plastic illuminated snail complete with lady rider wearing a large blue hat. Holding on with golden reins, and nudging one of the chandeliers, she occupies a position of honour in the centre of the room. But perhaps only the French could get away with it. Snails cooked in six different ways or as a *cassoulette* can also be ordered from the menu.

In fairness, the service is far from snail-like, and I once ate a memorable *gratin de Saint Jacques au coulis d'érevisses* served on a bed of grated mushrooms, which made me want to return. They are, in fact, surprisingly good on fish, the *turbot Montorgueil* (stuffed with salmon) is a speciality, and the wine list is good on champagne and white wines; they even serve the former *en carafe* if required.

Crowded at lunchtime, it is more a place to go in the evening, and it has the advantage of being open on Sundays.

10 Rue de Richelieu
Tel: 42.96.09.17
Cards: AE, DC, VISA
Closed: Saturday,
Sunday, August
Nearest Metro: Palais-
Royal (1, 7)
Map ref: 3

Conveniently situated for the hotels around the Palais-Royal area and the Comédie Fran-çaise, *Pierre Traiteur* nevertheless attracts a faithful clientèle of regulars, many from the theatre itself, happy to bask in the warmth of its welcome and home cooking from the Auvergne.

In the days when Curnonsky 'discovered' it, Mère Nouyrigat used to be in the kitchen, and there is a story that one day in 1928 a certain Monsieur Martin went there to lunch and so enjoyed his meal that he dined at the same table every day it was open for the next forty years, never growing tired of the *charcuteries 'maison'* (including parslied ham from Burgundy and pork liver pâté), the *macquereau au cidre, foie gras en terrine*, the *boudin* with onions, *rognon de veau aux échalotes confites*, or the chocolate cream puffs.

Sadly, Mère Nouyrigat is no longer with us, but her son, Guy, carries on the tradition, aided by Marc Faucheux in the kitchen. There is still a classic menu card written out in purple ink, with a list of wines on the side, which somehow sets the tone of the restaurant as soon as you see it. A fuller wine list is presented as a matter of course, but you can happily settle for the white Vouvray or the red Bourgueil from the Loire, perhaps even a Beaujolais, all of which will go well with the food.

The *estofinade rouergate* (a fish stew) is spoken of in awe by aficionados – *Gault-Millau* go so far as to say the cod puts all the sea bass and lobsters in creation to shame – as is the *gratin Dauphinois*, separately, but not together!

The service is extremely kind and helpful, and like Monsieur Martin one can easily dine there alone.

Chez la Vieille. 37 Rue d l'Arbre-Sec. **Tel:** 42.60.15.78. **Cards:** None. **Closed:** Saturday, Sunday, August. Lunches only. **Nearest Metro:** Pont Neuf (7). **Map ref:** 4.

A convenient place to go after a hard morning's shopping at La Samaritaine, but you will need to book, for the restaurant is very small and Madame Biasin rarely removes her *'complet'* sign from the door. The menu for the day is recited by the waitress and if you catch the words *'pot-au-feu'*, that is a dish to be recommended. There is a fixed-price menu with service included.

Au Pied de Cochon. 6 Rue Coquillière. **Tel:** 42.36.11.75. **Cards:** AE, DC, VISA. **Open:** 24 hours a day every day. **Nearest Metro:** Les Halles (4). **Map ref:** 5.

One of a row of restaurants situated at the back of the new Les Halles, the etchings on the walls serve as reminders of what it was like in the old days. If you like pork, try the *Saint-Antoine* – a plate consisting of most of its extremities. *Au Pied de Cochon* belongs to the Blanc family, who also own *Le Grand Café* in the 9th arrondissement and *L'Alsace* in the 8th, so the quality of the ingredients is assured.

2ᵉ ARRONDISSEMENT

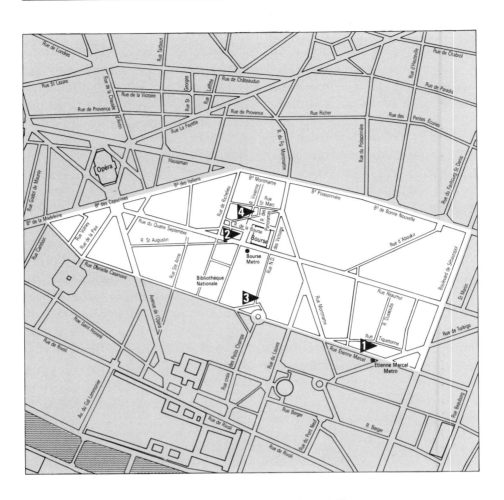

1. Les Paves de Tiquetonne
2. Le Vaudeville
3. Au Petit Pères
4. Le Petit Coin de la Bourse

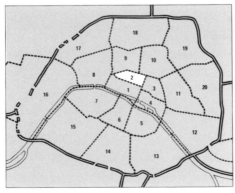

Pigeons don't really inspire great love – not even amongst each other if the number of rebuffs male pigeons have to suffer when they go in search of their oats is anything to go by. One lean winter, Ernest Hemingway, looking for something more sustaining than cereals, took to lying in wait for them in the Luxembourg Gardens, popping their still warm corpses into the pram alongside one-year-old Mr Bumby.

The pigeons outside the Sentier Metro station fare better. Every afternoon at four o'clock a little old lady arrives with a carrier bag full of food. The result makes Hitchcock's *The Birds* look like a budgerigars' tea party at the zoo; it is nature in the raw, feathers fly and it is every bird for itself. Needless to say, she isn't very popular with the locals, nor with the Club des Pigeons Citadins, who in other parts of the city are busy administering the supply of contraceptive grain in an effort to prevent such orgiastic scenes.

Around Sentier there is a certain amount of rawness about life as applied to human beings as well, for it is the centre of the Paris rag trade. If you want to begin the day with a mini-splash, then on the second floor of No. 65 Rue Montmartre, it is possible to buy last year's Yves Saint-Laurent model dresses and outfits with the original label at wholesale prices less 50%. But if you are an accompanying male, beware – the whole floor is one vast changing-room and everywhere you try not to look you encounter ladies in their bras, or less. Not that anyone seems to care two hoots, or coos if you related them to the pigeons outside the Metro station, for their behaviour is very similar. A sobering experience.

Ladies wearing even less, but without the benefit of 50% off for last year's models, can be seen displaying their wares *en masse* along the Rue St Denis at practically any hour of the day or night. Between there and the Sentier Metro station is a world of narrow streets full of sweat shops and little establishments tucked away in alleys. *Entrée* to this one may be *libre*, but if you happen to be carrying a camera then you are an object of immediate suspicion. Could it be that next season's fashions lie beyond this doorway, or is there some darker reason?

The 2nd arrondissement has seen a revival in recent years of many of the old passages which proliferated in the area before the rise of the great department stores, and were then left to decay. They are seductive places, with their glass roofs and little specialist shops and quiet cafés, especially on a rainy day when you have all the benefits of window shopping without the hustle and bustle of somewhere like the Boulevard Haussman.

One such is the Passage des Panoramas which runs from No. 11 Rue Montmartre through to Rue St Marc, with its tea rooms, antique shops and boutiques, and where the firm of Stern still carry out hand engraving and sell suitably elegant notepaper to match.

Near the Richelieu-Drouot Metro station, connecting the Boulevard des Italiens with the Rue de Richelieu is the Passage des Princes, which is worth a detour, not only for its recently renovated ironwork and tiled floor, but more especially for a look at the shopfront and through the windows of the old pipemaking firm of J. Sommer. There you see craftsmen at work, sculpting pipes in clay and fashioning others in briar and meerschaum for connoisseur smokers, just as they have done since 1855.

Head south down the Rue de Richelieu and then left into the Rue du Quatre Septembre and the Bourse looms into view. There are guided tours every forty minutes, but be warned – they take one and a half hours, including a film show. Brief views of the goings-on can be

had from another gallery; almost as dispiriting in its way as any Stock Exchange, except that it's in French and therefore less comprehensible.

South again, down the Rue Notre-Dame-des-Victoires takes you to the Place des Petits-Pères and the Basilica of Notre-Dame-des Victoires, scene of an annual pilgrimage to the Virgin. Inside, the walls are covered by some 30,000 plaques bearing the names of past sinners. It has a fine organ loft and seventeenth-century panelling, as well as seven paintings by Van Loo and a monument to the composer Lully.

The tiny Rue Vide Gousset (Pickpocket Street) joins the Place des Petits-Pères with the Place des Victoires. Westwards along La Feuillade and then the Rue des Petits Champs is the Bibliothèque Nationale, with its nine million books dating from the fifteenth century, and vast collection of medals, coins, cameos and other antiques. The entrance is in the Rue de Richelieu opposite a little park with an enormous Visconti fountain. Certain parts are open to the public, including the impressive Mazarin Gallery at the top of the Great Staircase.

On a more earthy level, Paul Corcelet at No. 46 Rue des Petits Champs is famous for his rare and exotic gastronomic products, like python stew (tinned), elephants' trunks and chestnuts in whisky and chocolate, to name but a few, and is also good for tea, mustard and vinegar in many varieties.

Crossing over the Avenue de l'Opéra, the Petits Champs becomes the Rue Danielle Casanova before joining up with the Rue de la Paix, and if you go window shopping along this most elegant of streets, it's worth remembering that on the first floor of No. 16 is Michel Swiss, where there are several rooms displaying perfume, leather goods, ties and cashmere sweaters, all marked down, when you come to pay, by 25% of the manufacturer's recommended price. (20% for credit cards)

If by now you are weighed down by all the perfume, ties, Yves Saint-Laurent dresses, not to mention elephants' trunks and meer-schaum pipes, there is always Harry's Bar at 'sank roo doe Noo' (5 Rue Daunou), once Clancey's Bar in New York and transferred lock, stock and barrel by jockey Tod Stone. Birthplace of the 'White Lady', 'Sidecar' and 'Bloody Mary', and headquarters of the IBF (Inter-national Bar Flies). There you can order a drink, close your eyes, and pretend you are back in the days when Gershwin was composing 'An American in Paris' while swopping drinks with Scott Fitzgerald and Hemingway, or you can simply listen to the piano in the cellar. (Closed on Christmas Day)

Alternatively, you can cheat a little and cross over the border into the 9th arrondissement at the Place de l'Opéra and take coffee or drink tea at that most famous of meeting places, the *Café de la Paix*. They even serve genuine old-fashioned lemonade between 15.00 and 18.00 each day.

17 Rue Tiquetonne
Tel: 42.36.18.93
Cards: AE, DC, VISA
Closed: Saturday lunch, Sunday
Nearest Metro: Étienne Marcel (4)
Map ref: 1

An unusual restaurant for Paris, for it could quite well be 'English Amateur' – until you taste the food, which is country-style Norman. To add to the feeling Monsieur Leconte-Ducroux takes the orders with a slightly absent-minded, apologetic air. Madame Leconte-Ducroux is responsible for the cooking; *hochepot de Grandmère aux pâtés fraîches, matelotte de lapin au boudin noir* – a delicious marriage – and *le pavé de Tiquetonne*, an enormous square of underdone beef in pastry, are among her specialities for the main course.

To start with there are stuffed mushrooms with cucumber mousse, multicoloured salad with haddock, Sancerre ham smoked over vine leaves, or goat cheese tart with mint sauce. To finish, there is another speciality – *soupe Normande* – a zabaglione of white cheese and beaten white of egg with calvados, or you can make do with homemade quince curd, chocolate fondant or walnut charlotte.

The wine list is short and not particularly cheap for what there is.

The dining-room is in a stone-walled basement, with candle-lit tables. At the rear there is a room set aside for a display of modern paintings. There is unobtrusive background music; an interesting mixture of jazz and classical music chosen from an enormous pile of records by the bar, which presumably reflect the taste of the owner.

Home cooking of a high order, with meat taking precedence over fish.

29 Rue Vivienne
Tel: 42.33.39.31
Cards: AE, CB, DC
Closed: Always open
Nearest Metro:
Bourse (3)
Map ref: 2

Le Vaudeville is very French, very Parisian, very authentic, and consequently very busy, so it is wise either to go early or to book. It belongs to Jean-Claude Bucher, who owns the highly successful *Brasserie Flo*, *Brasserie Julien* and *Terminus Nord*, which means you know exactly what to expect, for Monsieur Bucher has his finger firmly on the pulse of the city's gastronomic needs. Over three thousand customers every day of the year can't be wrong.

The surroundings, as with all his restaurants, are in tune with the feeling of nostalgia which seems to be currently in the air – *Le Vaudeville* is on the site of the old theatre where *La Dame aux Camelias* was first performed – and the art deco interior reflects the fact. Outside there are the ubiquitous stalls of shellfish, presided over by men in blue overalls hard at work with their knives. Inside, a highly professional, smartly-dressed, polite and exceedingly efficient staff serve generous portions of food from an unashamedly classical menu – *coq au vin*, *cassoulet*, lobster, vast plates of shellfish, sole; all accompanied by sound, reasonably priced wines served in quarter, half or litre carafes or by the bottle.

The tables are close together, so it isn't the place to go for a quiet *tête-à-tête*; a noisy one perhaps, for everyone else is so busy eating they haven't time for more than a passing glance at their neighbours, let alone listen to their conversation. At lunchtime it is popular with members of the Bourse opposite, and in the evening it caters for the before and after theatre trade. The bill comes promptly; clearly typed, exactly itemized and very reasonable. Long may Monsieur Bucher reign, for his restaurants are hard to fault.

Aux Petits Pères. 8 Rue Notre-Dame-des-Victoires. **Tel:** 42.60.91.73. **Cards:** AE, VISA. **Closed:** Saturday, Sunday, August. **Nearest Metro:** Bourse (3). **Map ref:** 3.

In contrast to the *Escargot Montorgueil* in the 1st arrondissement, *Gault-Millau* make no mention of this restaurant while *Michelin* award it a star, and as the décor is not the most notable feature of *Aux Petits Pères*, it must say something about the two guides.

It is, in fact, very much a Michelin restaurant, solid and reliable, offering dishes like *St Jacques à la provençale* and *faisan* according to season, and *ris de veau toulousaine* or *pintade aux choux*. Quiet in the evenings.

Le Petit Coin de la Bourse. 16 Rue Feydeau. **Tel:** 45.08.00.08. **Cards:** AE, DC, VISA. **Closed:** Saturday, Sunday. **Nearest Metro:** Bourse (3). **Map ref:** 4.

Another restaurant popular with stockbrokers anxious to recharge their batteries. A small, bistro-type establishment with interesting food making much use of whatever is available on the day. Classic cooking with a good value fixed-price menu inclusive of wine and service. Recommended.

3ᵉ ARRONDISSEMENT

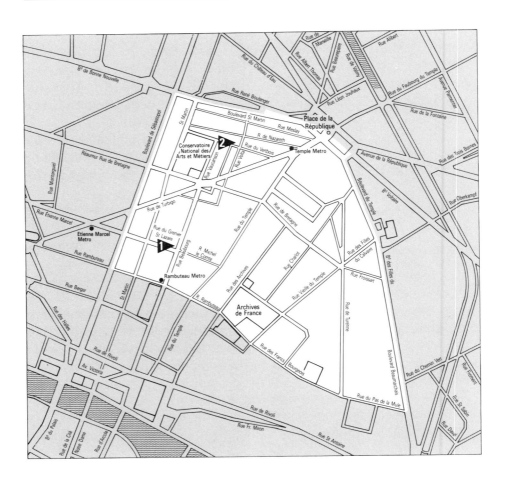

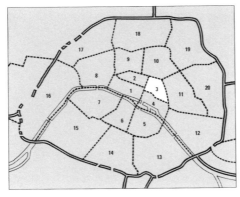

1. Ambassade d'Auvergne
2. L'Ami Louis

It is only right and proper that the Museum of French History should be situated at No. 60 Rue des Francs-Bourgeois, itself one of the oldest areas of Paris. The northern half of the Marais, with its scores of magnificent *hôtels* dotted about amongst narrow streets and *impasses*, accounts for most of the 3rd arrondissement.

Apart from the Musée de l'Histoire de France, where many great historical documents are on display, the Soubise Palace contains the National Archives – 6,000 million items spread over 175 miles of

The Soubise Palace – home of the National Archives.

shelving and now overflowing into the Hôtel de Rohan and other nearby buildings. The Rococo apartments of the Prince and Princess of Soubise can also be visited.

There is no better way of getting the 'feel' of the Marais as it must have been in days gone by than that provided by the Musée Carnavalet at No. 23 Rue de Sévigné, with its gardens and cloistered walks.

Almost like a museum within a museum, the Hôtel Carnavalet is worth a visit in its own right, but over and above that room after room is filled with memories of the past; old tradesmen's signs, antique furniture and models of the quarter as it was in the seventeenth and eighteenth centuries. Some of the rooms have been transferred *en bloc* from other *hôtels* in the area, as have a number of façades outside, notably the Nazarene arch, which once spanned the Rue des Francs-Bourgeois, and the Pavillon de Choiseul.

An early owner of the Hôtel was a certain Monsieur de Kernevenoy, a Breton nobleman whose name gradually became changed to Carnavalet, hence the name of the museum and the carnival mask over the entrance.

The Hôtel Carnavalet is literally surrounded by other *hôtels*; the Hôtel Salé, at 5 Rue de Thorigny is another which acquired its name as a kind of joke, for it was once the home of a salt tax collector. It is now a Picasso Museum containing a splendidly vast collection of the artist's works – many of which are on show for the first time, having

The Cloisters of the Hôtel Carnavalet.

been accepted by the State in lieu of death duties; the Hôtel Liberal-Bruand, at 1 Rue de la Perle, houses the Bricard Museum, which is devoted to locks, keys and other metalwork door funiture from Roman times onwards (closed Mondays, Tuesdays, holidays and August); the Hôtel du Grand Veneur – Master of the Royal Hunt House, at 60 Rue Turenne, has a façade displaying a boar's head and other symbols of the hunt, whilst inside is a magnificent grand staircase decorated with trophies and weapons, but you need to apply to the caretaker in order to see it.

Further north, at 270 Rue St Martin, in buildings which once belonged to the Saint-Martin-des-Champs priory, is the Musée National des Techniques; a wonderful collection of mechanical and electrical paraphernalia which traces the evolution of science and technology from the seventeenth century until the present day. The collection is so vast that only a small part can be on display at any one time, and the museum is awaiting transfer to premises at La Vedette when the new complex has been completed. Items to be seen include old cars, aeroplanes, bicycles galore, Pascal's adding machine, Amédée Bollée's steam-powered car, antique clocks, the Lumière brothers' camera, a collection of mechanical toys, and many things to do with astronomy, optics, tele-communications and radio, steel-making, spinning and weaving; nothing is left out and there is something for everyone. (Open every day except holidays – noon to 17.45, Sundays, when entry is free, 10.00 to 17.30)

Near the Beaubourg, at 23 Rue Beaubourg, one can see mechanical contraptions of a more plebeian, although no less interesting kind. The Las Vegas Museum contains some 150 exhibits culled from the amusement arcades of Europe and America, fruit machines, try-your-strength machines, machines for telling your fortune; there is even a vertical roulette wheel which once amused impatient patrons of a bordello at the Place des Ternes.

Well worth a visit while you are in the area in the Musée de la Musique Mécanique. In a little house at the end of the Impasse Berthaud, close to the Rambuteau Metro station, the owners lavish love and affection on their amazing collection of mechanical instruments and then communicate it to others in easily understandable French between the hours of 14.00 and 19.00 each Saturday, Sunday and *Fêtes* days throughout the year.

Here you can see early phonographs, pianolas – including one for which both Debussy and Stravinsky played special works, mechanical violins, music boxes, a life-size piano accordionist and drummer, organs, polyphons, even a man who catches endless potatoes in his mouth, all in perfect working order. The tour lasts an hour and a quarter and a thoroughly good time is had by all.

22 Rue du Grenier-St-Lazare
Tel: 42.72.31.22
Cards: VISA
Closed: Sunday
Nearest Metro: Rambuteau (11) Etienne Marcel (4)
Map ref: 1

As might be expected, the ambience and cooking (by the owner's son-in-law) are of the Massif Central. The décor is massive too; oak beams are festooned with mouth-watering mountain hams, wrought-iron chandeliers hang from the ceiling; all very rustic, and you know you are in for a good feed.

As a first course, *soupe aux choux gratinées* is not for the faint-hearted – especially if you plan to follow it with *saucisse* and *aligot* – which puts one in a bit of a quandary to start with, for if you haven't tried it before, the *aligot* is a must. Made with potatoes, cream, garlic and Cantal cheese whipped in a copper pan, it is far removed from the 'mashed potato' of one's childhood. On the other hand, *boudin noir* served with a mound of chestnuts is another speciality, which could be preceded by *salade de cabécous rôtis* – grilled goat cheese on a bed of greens. But would that leave room for the generous portion of *oeufs à la neige*?

In short, planning a meal at the *Ambassade d'Auvergne* needs a certain amount of careful thought, and it doesn't do any harm to go into training beforehand.

One is helped by a menu which lists daily specialities: Monday – *pot-au-feu*; Tuesday – duck stew; Wednesday – meat and vegetable soup; Thursday – *cassoulet*; Friday – *estouffade* (a meat stew); Saturday – *chou farci*.

Recently there have been one or two concessions to nouvelle cuisine, but on the whole it is a place for serious trenchermen and women who like getting value for money and seldom go away feeling disappointed.

There are delicious Auvergnat cheeses if you can bring yourself to face them, and the wine list includes many examples of good country wines such as Chateaugay red and Saint Pourçain white, which are a perfect accompaniment to the food.

An ideal place to go on a cold winter's evening, when the welcome will be as warm as the fire which burns in the grate.

32 Rue de Vertbois
Tel: 48.87.77.48
Cards: AE, DC, VISA
Closed: Monday,
Tuesday, July, August
Nearest Metro:
Temple (3)
Map ref: 2

Publishing being the long drawn-out business that it is, one almost hesitates to include *L'Ami Louis*, for Monsieur Antoine Magnin, the *patron*, is fast approaching his ninetieth year. Well, no faster than the rest of us, it's just that much closer, and when he hangs up his apron for the last time, the world – including a nearby home for stray dogs who benefit from any left-overs at the end of the day – will be a great deal poorer.

You enter a long room, dark with age, the walls and ceiling of which haven't seen a decorator's brush for many a year. Little oval mirrors line the walls and there are coat-hooks beside each iron-legged table. A giant stove with matching pipes and a display of the day's fresh fruit and vegetables complete the décor. At the far end of the room there is a serving hatch beyond which Monsieur Magnin can be seen working away in front of a wood-burning oven, preparing the roasts which are his speciality.

The welcome is perfunctory, but if you work on the waiters and they see you are enjoying your meal, as indeed you will, they quickly thaw. You order wine, the cork is drawn and sniffed, the glasses filled; to offer it for tasting would be an affront to the waiter's professional pride. You eat with implements, and if there are two of you and one orders *escargots* the other is brought tongs and a fork automatically, because you will of course wish to share them. The helpings are copious.

If it should come to pass that I am ever asked what I would like for my last meal on earth, I would go to *L'Ami Louis* and order his beautiful Bayonne ham, which arrives along with toasted slices of *baguette* and unsalted butter. Then I would plump for roast chicken, which has to be the best ever, and comes with *pommes frites*. To end with, another speciality – *nougatine* – a delicious chocolate-covered tartlet which is one of the patron's inventions. Accompanied by a Brouilly perhaps, or if it really was one's last meal and one felt like splashing out, a modest Bordeaux – like a Château Frombauge, I would die a happy man. And if I was lucky enough to be granted a reprieve I wouldn't be able to eat again that day anyway.

4^e ARRONDISSEMENT

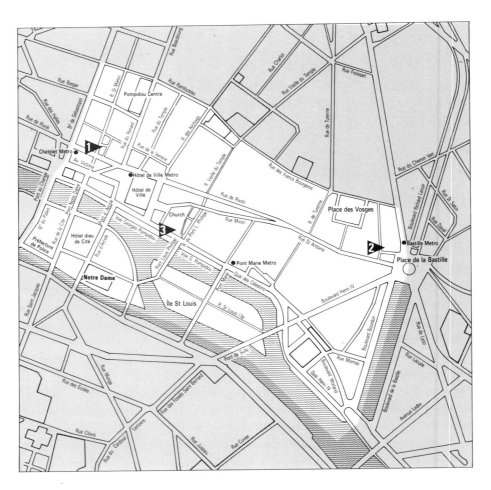

1. Benoit
2. Bofinger
3. Au Quai des Ormes

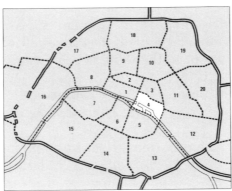

Uncompromisingly stark and modern, looking from a distance like a disembowelled oil refinery, the Centre National d'Art et de Culture George Pompidou, popularly known as the 'Beaubourg', was conceived as a fun centre aimed at bringing art to the people.

Behind all the pipes and tubes, there is an Industrial Design Centre; a photographic gallery; a large library with audio and visual facilities; a children's play centre; a branch of the Cinémathèque

The Georges Pompidou Centre.

Française with its own cinema; and on the third, fourth and fifth floors, fulfilling its prime function, the largest collection of contemporary art in the world. You can also buy art books and posters on the ground floor, and on the top floor there is a restaurant and a self-service snack bar with fine views over Paris.

Outside on the vast piazza, fire-eaters, poets, mime artists and hypnotists perform, assured of an audience whatever they do, for in terms of visitors the Beaubourg is undeniably successful, having long ago overtaken the Eiffel Tower as the number one most visited Parisian tourist attraction.

Notre-Dame cathedral, with a view of its 50 ft high flying buttresses and the magnificent spire which rises nearly 300 ft into the air.

At the other end of the arrondissement, and in total contrast to the Beaubourg, stands Notre-Dame, harmonious, balanced and indestructible.

Unlike the Beaubourg, which is already showing signs of wear and tear, not to mention rust, Notre-Dame has withstood wars and revolutions and the ravages of time and tourists for over 800 years. It has been pillaged and ransacked, suffered the whitewashing of its walls and replacing of many of its stained-glass windows with plain glass in order to let in more light; seen its statuary destroyed and its great bell melted down during the Revolution; been used as a food store, and during the Commune of 1871 had a bonfire made of its seating.

Then in 1831, publication of Victor Hugo's book *Notre-Dame de Paris* (known in English as *The Hunchback of Notre-Dame*) triggered off a wave of enthusiasm for its restoration, and in 1845 the architect Viollet-le-Duc set about the mammoth task which was to take twenty-five years.

Since pagan times people have worshipped on the spot where

Notre-Dame now stands. It was once the site of a Roman temple dedicated to Jupiter, and in front of the west door there is a brass plaque marking the spot from which all distances to Paris are measured. Consequently it is the very centre of the French universe.

There is so much of historical interest spiralling out from Notre-Dame; ancient bridges and *quais*; the Law Courts; the Hôtel Dieu, with its adjacent flower market which becomes a bird market on Sundays; it is hard to know where to start or what to leave in or take out. In the end the only solution is to take your favourite guide-book firmly in the hand and set out on a voyage of exploration. It could take a day, or a week, or a whole lifetime; the choice is yours.

On a completely different, down-to-earth level, opposite the Hôtel de Ville in the Place of the same name (once the Place de Grève and the gathering place of unemployed Parisians — hence the word grève — a strike) stands the Bazaar de l'Hôtel de Ville, the basement of which no home handy-man should fail to visit, for it is jam-packed with everything one could possibly need, in every possible size. It is quite unique.

To the east of the Pompidou Centre lies the southern half of Le Marais, one of the most attractive of the old quarters of Paris, and a fascinating area to explore, from the Temple des Billettes with its ancient cloisters, through the Jewish quarter with its kosher food shops and synagogues, to the Place des Vosges, which received its name because the Vosges area of France was always first to pay its taxes.

As the name suggests, Le Marais was once marshland, and it wasn't until the twelfth century that it was first drained and made habitable. In the beginning it was the site for various religious communities and monasteries, reminders of which can still be seen in many of the street names. It was in the fifteenth century that it started to become fashionable and the building of the many great mansions began. By the eighteenth century, however, a decline had set in and with the storming of the nearby Bastille on 14 July 1789, the last of the wealthy moved out, leaving it to the poor of Paris who not surprisingly allowed it to deteriorate.

The decline lasted until the nineteen sixties, when the ever-enlightened André Malraux stepped in and declared it a conservation area, thus preventing its wholesale destruction. A great deal of restoration work has since taken place and it has become fashionable again, but sadly many of the old craftsmen — the watchmakers, the repairers of stringed instruments, woodworkers and others, are being edged out.

And if you end up in the Place des Vosges, what better way of rounding things off than by taking tea beneath one of the shady arcades which surround this almost perfect square? Perhaps at one of the cafés patronized by Inspector Maigret when he and Madame Maigret lived there. You, too, can make mental notes about the goings-on all around as he once did in 'Madame Maigret's Admirer'.

Looking out from the tomb of the Unknown Deportee.

Returning to the Ile de la Cité, on the easternmost tip, at the end of a little garden in the Square Jean XXIII, is an underground memorial to the 20,000 French people who died in Nazi camps during the last war: the Mémorial de la Déportation. Everything is starkly simple; a few concrete cells, some chains; no names, only a list of the many camps inscribed on the walls; and the tomb of the 'Unknown Deportee'.

It is impossible not to be moved by it.

The Pont St Louis, leading from the Square Jean XXIII takes you to Paris's other island, the Ile St Louis. Originally there were two islands, the Ile aux Vaches, and the Ile Notre Dame, both belonging to the Canons of Notre Dame who used them for grazing their cattle, renting out the rest to local washerwomen and fishermen. Then, in the early seventeenth century, the Crown gave Christophe Marie – an architect/surveyor – permission to develop the site provided he turned the two islands into one and built a bridge to connect it with the right bank – hence the name Pont Marie.

The whole project took around fifty years to complete and could be called Paris's first piece of real estate. It accounts for the planned feel of the criss-crossed streets and the harmonious nature of the architecture. Apart from an ever-present parking problem, which makes one wonder if the residents ever dare take their cars anywhere for fear of never getting back again, it must look very much as it did three hundred years ago. The seventeenth-century houses lining the streets and *quais*, with their courtyards hidden behind enormous studded doors, many still with mounting blocks behind, left over from the days of horse-drawn carriages, all blend together in a way which doesn't always happen in other parts of Paris which evolved over a much longer period of time.

The little parish church, St Louis en l'Ile, with its unusual iron clock and pierced spire, lends a provincial air to the scene and one might easily be in any small French town rather than the heart of the capital. The inside of the church is a good example of Baroque architecture and also contains a plaque from the city of St Louis, Missouri, which took its name.

Not surprisingly, the island has always attracted writers and artists in search of peace and quiet, and over the years the Hôtel du Lauzun, at 17 Quai d'Anjou, was home to the poets Gautier, Rilke and Baudelaire as well as Sickert and Wagner. It now belongs to the State and is used to accommodate important guests. Another mansion, the Hôtel Lambert, at 2 Rue St Louis-en-l'Ile, is where Voltaire lived with his mistress, the Marquise de Châtelet. Considered the finest private house in the whole of Paris, it now belongs to Guy de Rothschild. During the last war it was a transit point for escaping Allied airmen shot down over France.

But life on the Ile St-Louis is not lived entirely behind closed doors. There are the quais with their *clochards* and fishermen and lovers strolling hand in hand, and there are lots of small shops and cafés. At number 35 Rue St Louis-en-l'Ile, is the aptly named Librairie Ulysse, a travel bookshop whose doorway window is always lined with cards from people seeking lifts to unlikely far-off places like Katmandu. If you hanker after a cup of tea, then the Salon de Thé St Louis, at No. 81, will offer you a choice of over fifty different varieties. Berthillon, at No. 31, sells the best ice-cream in Paris. They are sufficiently established and confident of their success to close on Mondays, Tuesdays and all through August. There is usually a queue and on a busy day it can take up to half an hour to get served. At such times it is better to take a stroll round to Le Flore en l'Ile, at 42 Quai d'Orléans, where they serve the same ice-cream, provide you with things to read and, if you are lucky enough to get a seat in their window, throw in a lovely view of Notre-Dame for free.

20 Rue St-Martin
Tel: 42.72.25.76
Cards: None
Closed: Saturday,
Sunday, August
Nearest Metro:
Châtelet (1, 4, 7)
Map ref: 1

Worth a visit if only for the home-made *boudin* with apples, but there is much more besides; beef and brawn salad, hot sausage and bacon salad, sauté of lamb, *soupe de moules* and *boeuf mode braisé bourgeoise* – two of the dishes which earned them a star in *Michelin*, – duckling with turnips; all of which can be washed down with good Beaujolais especially bottled for the owner, or a more expensive Burgundy if you feel so inclined.

The cuisine is bourgeois Lyonnaise, and as you squeeze into your seat between the potted palms and gaze round at the other tables with their spotless white cloths and view the old photographs on the walls you could well be back in the early part of the century when the restaurant was first opened. It is the kind of establishment that makes your taste buds throb with anticipation of good things to come.

Pleasantly situated on the corner of what is now a quiet pedestrian precinct alongside the little church of St Merri (the north-west tower of which houses the oldest bell in Paris), *Benoit* is to the right bank what *Allard* is to the left. Popular with businessmen at lunchtime and with French families in the evening, so you will need to book.

5 Rue de la Bastille
Tel: 42.72.87.82
Credit Cards: AE, DC, EC, VISA
Closed: Always open
Nearest Metro: Bastille (1, 5, 8)
Map ref: 2

Connoisseurs of bizarre tastes in interior decoration returning from a safari along the western end of Rue de Faubourg St Antoine with its never-ending display of all that is worst in French interior décor, unsure if they will ever be able to look an elephant straight in the eye again without wondering if it will suddenly turn into a cocktail cabinet, can bring themselves slowly back down to earth again over a kir beneath the opulent stained-glass ceiling of *Bofinger*. Hidden away in a back-street on the west side of the vast Place de la Bastille, its extravagant but beautifully restored turn-of-the-century surroundings make it one of the handsomest brasseries in Paris.

If *Gault-Millau* have in the past been less than kind – 'the mirrors which softly reflect the copper pots and buttoned leather of the seats also reflect the somewhat discontented faces of the guests of M. Urtizverea, who expected something a bit better' – faith now seems to have been restored, another point awarded, and rightly so.

Apart from a good selection of sea-food, most of the specialities are Alsation; *sauerkraut* comes in every possible variation – the *boudins noirs* are good, as are the frankfurters. Also to be recommended is the *cassoulet* of beans, sausage and duck, and the *brandade* of salt cod puréed with olive oil. The house Riesling makes a good accompaniment. The service is brisk; the bill at the end not unreasonable.

72 Quai d l'Hôtel-de-Ville
Tel: 42.74.72.22
Cards: VISA
Closed: Saturday,
Sunday, First three weeks
in August
Nearest Metro: Hôtel-
de-Ville (1) Pont Marie
(1, 7)
Map ref: 3

On first entering, one feels *Au Quai des Ormes* doesn't quite match up to what the exterior has led one to expect. It is slightly formal without being unfriendly; the diners more dressed for the occasion than is often the case in France. Perhaps it is out of respect for the owner.

Monsieur Masraff hails from Cairo and gave up medicine to be a chef. On route to being a restaurateur he studied with the brothers Haeberlin and Troisgros, and did a spell in the kitchens at *Taillevant* before branching out on his own, first in Brittany, then in Paris. Such dedication suggests a striving after perfection; no bad thing in a chef. At any rate it has already won him a star in *Michelin* and two red toques in *Gault-Millau*, both of whom single out his very delicious *ravioli de champignons sauvages* and the hot and cold desserts.

Apart from the *carte*, there is a fixed-price menu with a choice of two different dishes for each course. There is also a separate menu for those on a diet (900 calories), which is worrying if you happen to be eating at the next table; it sets you totting up your own calorific intake, particularly if you happen to be enjoying another speciality – rabbit garnished with an assortment of wild mushrooms tucked up in a bed of pasta.

The wine list merits a separate folder and the prices are reasonable, although, as is so often the case in France, few of them are more than five or six years old. Before and after the meal there are titbits, and delicious chocolates arrive with the coffee. So much for the 900 calories.

Afterwards you can take a romantic stroll past the beautifully restored and floodlit church of Saint-Gervais-Saint-Protais, one glimpse of which, according to Voltaire, was enough to make anyone believe in God. (Turn left outside the restaurant, then left again.)

5e ARRONDISSEMENT

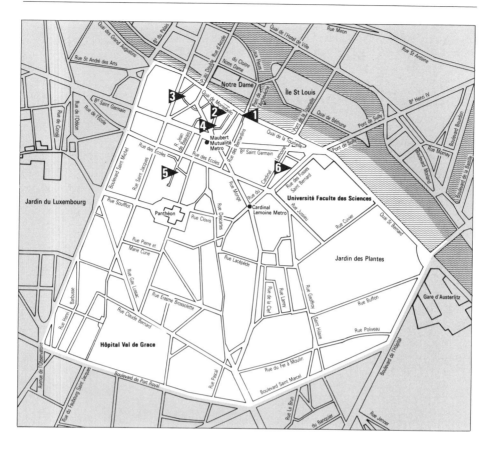

1. L'Ambroisie
2. Atelier Maître-Albert
3. Auberge des Deux Signes
4. Dodin-Bouffant
5. Le Coupe-Chou
6. Moissonnier

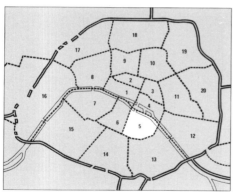

There are few bargains to be found in the green, zinc-topped stalls belonging to the *bouquinistes* who line the banks of the Seine, but hope springs eternal in the human breast and they are as much a part of the Paris scene as the Eiffel Tower and Folies-Bergère.

In 1822, when they were first given official recognition, there were only sixty-eight of them, now there are over three hundred. On the left bank they begin at the Quai de la Tournelle in the 5th arrondissement, where they specialize in detective stories and science fiction. Further along, on the Quai St Michel, it is mainly old

postcards and reproduction posters aimed at the tourists. Here, on the Quai Montebello, engravings and old books are the order of the day, most of them covered in plastic to protect them from the *fouillemerdes* – the browsers who come to handle but not to buy.

Traditionally thought of as the 'Latin Quarter', the 5th is much more than that. It is perhaps the most 'concentrated' of the arrondissements; certainly the most varied, and nowhere are both these aspects more in evidence than in the Rue Mouffetard – Hemingway's 'wonderful narrow crooked market street', which begins in the leafy Place de la Contrescarpe and winds its way down to the church of Saint-Médiard near the Censier Daubeton Metro station.

Originally part of a Roman road joining Lyon to the capital, it was once principally occupied by tanners and dyers – hence the name – *mouffette* being the French word for 'skunk'. Nowadays it is a

Tradesmen's Standards are an important feature of shops in the Rue Mouffetard.

The booksellers who line the quais of the Seine are as much a part of the Paris scene as the Eiffel Tower. With no overheads, able to open and close when they feel like it, they are a hardy breed of individualists.

bustling hotch-potch of races and colours and creeds, and you can buy anything there from fruit straight out of its crates to dried fish from North Africa and home-made pasta. On either side are numerous little shops and cafés, many with interesting signs hanging outside, like the one above.

If you happen to be there in the morning, it's useful to remember that *Le Moule à Gâteau* at No. 111 has superb *pain au chocolat* fresh from the oven, as well as many other delights.

The 5th also has the narrowest street in Paris – the Rue du Chat-qui-Pêche (off Rue de la Huchette); the Musée de Cluny at 6 Place Paul-Painlevé, with its collection of mediaeval treasures including the famous series of six tapestries depicting a lady with a unicorn; the Panthéon, that great mausoleum for the famous dead of France, containing in its crypt the tombs of Voltaire, Emile Zola, Victor

Hugo, Rousseau and Louis Braille; the beautifully decorated church of Saint-Séverin, where evening concerts are regularly held; and the Square René Viviani, with its seats and its view of Notre-Dame across the Seine, its ancient acacia tree, said to be the second oldest in Paris (the tallest is another acacia in the Jardin des Plantes) and, acting as a backcloth, the little Greek-Catholic church of St Julien-le-Pauvre.

The oldest complete church in Paris, St Julien-le-Pauvre, is also one of the simplest and prettiest. Collecting boxes abound, for it still has the needs of the poor at heart, and it is frequently used for pauper funerals.

Close by, at 37 Rue de la Bûcherie, is the English bookshop known as Shakespeare & Co. In the twenties and thirties it gained its reputation through being a meeting place for expatriate writers; Hemingway, Miller, Joyce, Pound, and many others. More than that, Sylvia Beach, the owner, often gave them free board and lodging. Nowadays the tradition is carried on by another American, George Whitman, and it is not uncommon to have to negotiate sleeping figures in order to reach the shelves in the rooms upstairs.

The Musée des Collections Historiques de la Préfecture de Police at 1 *bis* Rue des Carmes, may not sound like everyone's idea of an exciting afternoon out, but if you are at all interested in crime and punishment then it is worth a visit and is one of the few museums which is free (open 14.00–17.00 Wednesdays and Thursdays only). It is situated inside the 5th arrondissement police headquarters; a fact which seems to have escaped the notice of some of those who work there.

Underlying most of one's wanderings in the 5th is an awareness of the vast store of knowledge which has been accumulated and handed down over the years by the Sorbonne and its various faculties, and the Ancienne Ecole Polytechnique, which has been, and still is, responsible for supplying the élite of the French educational system to the government and the higher echelons of the Civil Service.

The Sorbonne was one of the greatest concentrated seats of learning in the world, a law unto itself until the fatal day in May 1968 when student uprisings caused the police to set foot inside its hallowed precincts for the first time in four hundred years. It was an act which later led to two noticeable reforms. The University system in France was changed, not the least in Paris, so that the Sorbonne is no longer the autonomous place it once was, but part of a series of buildings spread around the city; the other result was that the cobble-stones in the area were torn up and replaced by tarmac.

One wonders what this man is doing just inside the entrance to the Jardin des Plantes. Did he simply happen to find a piece of stone lying on the path, or did he bring it on a trolley from the Gare d'Austerlitz? And if he is setting up in business, why not use a smaller plinth so that he doesn't need to stand on a box to work?

Perhaps he has been commissioned by the powers that be to carve a bust in memory of Monsieur Buffon, naturalist and author of a vast Encyclopaedia of Natural History, who was Superintendent from 1739 until he died in 1788, and was largely responsible for the expansion of the gardens from a royal herb bed to their present size and importance.

One of the less fashionable of the Paris parks, and largely ignored by tourists, the Jardin des Plantes is a welcome oasis after the hustle and bustle of the rest of the 5th.

There is a small zoo – originally made up of a collection of animals transferred from Versailles during the Revolution, an aquarium, the Natural History Museum and various off-shoot galleries with permanent exhibitions relating to prehistoric monsters, insects, plant fossils and precious stones; a fine botanical garden with over 10,000 different plants, a herb garden and another devoted to alpine plants, a maze, the famous cedar of Lebanon, planted in 1734 by Bernard de Jussieu, who was reputed to have brought it back from Syria in his hat, keeping it alive with the aid of his daily water ration, but in fact got it from Kew Gardens; and in October, the Salon de Champignon.

It is an agreeable place for a stroll along the wide avenues with their overhanging trees, flanked on either side by flower beds and lawns dotted with modern statuary.

65 Quai de la Tournelle
Tel: 46.33.18.65
Cards: AE, CB, VISA
Closed: Sunday,
Monday, part of August
and holidays
Nearest Metro:
Maubert-Mutualité (10)
Map ref: 1

Small, modern – chrome and black leather seating – nothing out of place, with slightly austere service by matchingly handsome young waiters bearing food of a very high order.

L'Ambroisie received the plaudits of French food writers soon after it opened and shot to fame in the early eighties when it was besieged by press and television reporters lying in wait for Monsieur Mitterand, who lived nearby in the Rue de Bièvre and had just been made President.

Bernard Pacaud spent four years working for Claude Peyrot at the *Vivarois* before opening his own restaurant; a fact which is reflected in the style of cooking and in the constant striving after perfection. The menu is fairly short – in keeping with the number of tables. It lists three or four dishes each of fish and meat for the main course, with a larger selection of first courses, and perhaps in consequence all are cooked with elegance and finesse and are hard to fault.

Highly recommended are the *mousse de poivrons, panaché de poissons au safran, raie aux choux*, and, to follow, *mille-feuilles* with fruit of the season, or chocolate gâteau.

There is a good, catholic wine list.

It is not a cheap restaurant, but neither is it expensive for what you get, and at lunchtime there is a fixed-price menu. It's the kind of place for a special occasion. Because it is very tiny – at the time of writing there are only nine tables – it is very necessary to book ahead.

1 Rue Maître-Albert
Tel: 46.33.13.78
Cards: None
Closed: Lunchtime every day, Sunday, holidays
Nearest Metro: Maubert-Mutualité (10)
Map ref: 2

According to the dictionary, *atelier* means 'workshop', and certainly if it wasn't for the name painted above the doorway and windows one might easily direct one's gaze towards Notre-Dame on the opposite bank of the Seine, and walk past numbers 1–5 Rue Maître-Albert thinking the premises were devoted to the manufacture of light machinery, bedding, or some other product, which would be a great pity if you happened to be seeking a good meal at an extremely reasonable price.

The *Atelier Maître-Albert* doesn't appear in many guide books, and doesn't really need to, for it is well patronized by the French, who know a good thing when they see one.

Entering via the bar, you find yourself being led into a large, almost cavernous room, which is divided up into small areas without any obvious fixed kind of plan, so that the overall effect is much cosier than it might otherwise be. The large areas of stone walling are broken up by modern paintings and the ceiling by old beams, and in winter a log fire blazes away in a magnificent fireplace.

There is a fixed-price dinner menu (the restaurant isn't open for lunch), which includes six or seven different items under each heading; *boudin de poissons*, *jambon persillé*, *pigeonneaux*, *daube de canard*, *Meaux Brie* cheese, and sorbets from Berthillon have all been approved. Wine is included in the price; red, white or rosé – the equivalent of half a bottle per person, so that if there are two of you it will be, perhaps, a bottle of Chinon, suitably chilled, or a Gamay de Touraine.

It is usually crowded later in the evening, so you will either need to go early or book beforehand.

46 Rue Galande
Tel: 43.25.46.56
Cards: AC, DC, EC, VISA
Closed: Sunday, Holidays
Nearest Metro: Maubert-Mutualité (10)
Map ref: 3

If you are one of those people who dislike background music while you eat, then you may be put off when you first take your seat in one of the high-backed chairs of the *Auberge des Deux Signes* and adjust to the mediaeval surroundings of what was once part of the Priory of Saint Julien-le-Pauvre. This would be a pity, because there is nothing *pauvre* about the menu. Monsieur Dhulster hails from the Auvergne – a region of France which has produced more than its fair share of Paris restaurateurs and is known also for its breeding of perfectionists.

Anyway, the music is both discreet and classical, and if you are plucking up courage to complain, the wind is almost immediately taken out of your sails by the arrival of a large leather-bound list of items available, from which you may make a choice.

The food is a mixture of ancient and modern; little slivers of *jambon d'Auvergne* come with the apéritifs, and there are larger slices available on the menu as a first course as well. Butter arrives with the *Poilâne* bread. Between the first and second course a thimbleful of Vodka appears, rendering the palate in pristine condition for what is to follow, *sole meunière*, for example, or *pigeonneau en papillote*. Afterwards there is a *bavarois* flavoured with Souillac (a prune liqueur) or chocolate *mousse*. Other recommended dishes are: *civet de moules, foie de veau au vinaigre de Xères* and *Talmouse*, a tart of *fromage blanc*.

Entering the modern frontage from the Rue Galande doesn't prepare you for the view from inside the restaurant. On the ground floor there are tantalizing glimpses of trees in the garden of Saint Julien-le-Pauvre, and on the first floor Notre-Dame itself.

There is a good wine list, predominantly of red Bordeaux, but with other interesting items as well. Monsieur Dhulster is an attentive host and spends his mornings at the market selecting the freshest of ingredients.

A pleasant place to go for a romantic evening, and if things don't work out and the conversation flags, you can always order the 'Grand March' from *Aïda* or Beethoven's Ninth.

25–27 Rue Frédéric-Sauton
Tel: 43.25.25.14
Cards: DC, VISA
Closed: Saturday, Sunday, August, Christmas
Nearest Metro: Maubert-Mutualité (10)
Map ref: 4

Classic, popular, reliable, bustling, very Parisian; all of these things apply to the *Dodin-Bouffant*, where Jean-Marie Clément carries on a tradition in cooking set by Jacques Manière, who has recently retired to the country.

The emphasis is on fish. Oysters, mussels, clams and other denizens of the deep are taken from salt-water tanks in the basement to be served by themselves or as part of a magnificent *plateau des fruits de mer*. Also recommended is the *ragout de clams aux asperges*, *bar fumé* and steamed scallops with pasta, all of which can be accompanied by good, reasonably-priced wine. *Soufflés chaud aux fruits* are another speciality.

Le Coupe-Chou, 11 Rue Lanneau. **Tel:** 46.33.68.69. **Cards:** VISA. **Nearest Metro:** Maubert-Mutualité (10). **Map ref:** 5.

A popular place for late eating in an old house which was converted into a restaurant some years ago by a group of actors who were perhaps beguiled by the fact that the site was once the setting for the French equivalent of Sweeney Todd, the demon barber of Fleet Street; but don't let it put you off the paté or the duck with prunes and apples.

Moissonnier, 28 Rue des Fossés-St-Bernard. **Tel:** 43.29.87.65. **Cards:** None. **Closed:** Sunday dinner, Monday, August. **Nearest Metro:** Cardinal Lemoine (10). **Map ref:** 6.

An unchanging bistro serving food from the Lyon region in large portions to faithful customers, so you will need to book. Try the *carré d'agneau* or the *boudin noir*, but don't expect the former to be anything other than it should be – pink. A good assortment of cheese and wine from the area makes it a popular place for wine-merchants. What more recommendation do you need?

6ᵉ ARRONDISSEMENT

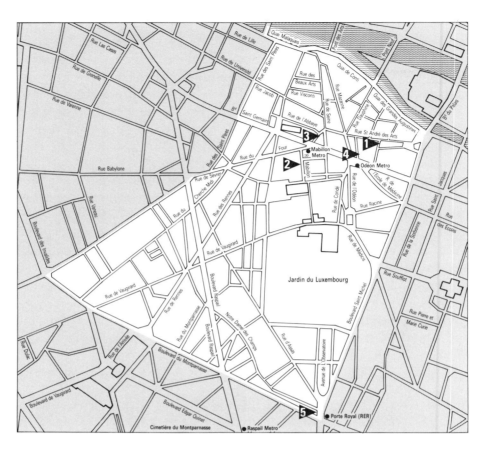

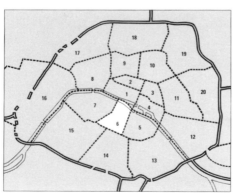

1. Allard
2. Aux Charpentiers
3. Le Petit Zinc
4. Le Procope
5. La Closerie des Lilas

Unless you want to buy olives – in which case Soleil de Provence at 6 Rue du Cherche-Midi has the best in Paris, grown on their own *Provençal* farm – or go shopping for books, records, cameras and hi-fi at the branch of FNAC at 136 Rue de Rennes, highly recommended for all these things at uninflated prices, then the area to the south and west of the Luxembourg Gardens doesn't have a great deal to offer.

But between the gardens and the Seine lies a whole world of bustling thoroughfares and interconnected narrow, winding streets steeped in history and in literary associations.

In the Jardin du Luxembourg old men play chess ... ... or sleep in the afternoon sun, dreaming of days gone by.

Children play with their boats ...
... or make new friends.

... While some are content simply to sit with their back against a tree, watching the world go by, dreaming of things to come.

Oscar Wilde died at 13 Rue des Beaux-Arts, now the very chic and expensive L'Hôtel. Wagner once lodged in the Rue Jacob, Longfellow in the Rue Racine. Sarah Bernhardt was born in the Rue de l'Ecole-de-Medicine, the same street where Marat was stabbed to death in his bath. Whistler lived for a while in Rue Bourbon-le-Château, and Beaumarchais wrote the book of The Barber of Seville in the Rue de Condé. Docteur Guillotin gave his name to a machine he invented in his workshop at Cour du Commerce St-André, and Rue Mazarine, now full of rare book shops, apartment houses and antique sellers, was once a popular site for indoor tennis courts, some of which were later turned into theatres; Paris saw its first opera performed at No. 42.

More recently, Gertrude Stein lived with her paintings at 5 Rue Christine, looked after by her friend, Alice B. Toklas, who wrote a cookery book based on her experiences, and for a while in the post-war years it was the haunt of Brigitte Bardot, Juliette Greco and Françoise Sagan.

It is a world of publishers and booksellers, art galleries, tiny specialist firms, bookbinders, food shops, and small hotels with matching bedrooms covered in flowered wallpaper, bidets on rails, and *minuterie* switches on the stairs and landings to save the light being left on when the occupants return late.

It is the Boulevard St Germaine, with its cafés, like *Les Deux Magots*, *Le Flore* and *Lipp*, where ideas have been born and cross-fertilized and argued over, populated over the years by intellectuals living in hotels and apartments by night and in the cafés by day. What singled out particular establishments in the first place is hard to say; although who went where was always important. *Lipp* has always been favoured by politicians and celebrities, as you may well discover when you arrive; there is a distinct pecking order in the seating arrangements. *Les Deux Magots* and *Le Flore* attract the literary set. The former was favoured by André Gide, Joyce, Ford Madox Ford and many American expatriates like Hemingway, John Dos Passos, and Ezra Pound. *Le Flore* received the custom of Simone de Beauvoir, Camus, Picasso and people from the world of film. Jean-Paul Sartre, after he moved north during the war from the Boulevard du Montparnasse, divided his time between the two, using the tables as his work desk while he held court to his disciples and gave birth to Existentialism.

Les Deux Magots is still a good place in which to have breakfast, and to look out across the square at the bell tower belonging to the oldest church in Paris, St Germaine-des-Près. The church itself was originally part of a Benedictine Abbey so vast it had a moat which reached as far as the Seine. Sipping hot chocolate, it is hard to picture the area as having once been a place where justice was dispensed in public on the gibbet and pillory and where, in 1557, two Huguenots had their tongues torn out before being burned alive for meeting in secret.

The Place St Germain with the church beyond. Once the scene of incredible atrocities, now a good place to take coffee.

Not far away, at the top of a narrow staircase in Rue de Furstenberg, is the studio where Delacroix lived and worked. It is now a museum (closed on Tuesdays) and is worth a visit, not only because it has been kept as it was, with displays of letters, drawings, sketches and personal belongings, and for constantly changing exhibitions devoted to particular aspects of his work, but also for the little garden behind – perhaps not up to Monet's standards, but peaceful nonetheless.

For lovers of Delacroix's work, the church of Saint Sulpice, south of the Boulevard Saint Germain, has two frescoes, painted over a long period of time while he received inspiration from the services. Another interesting feature of the church is a bronze bar laid in the floor of the transept. Running in a line from north to south, it leads to a marble obelisk with an inset graduated brass scale which is illuminated by the rays of the sun at exactly midday during the equinoxes and solstices. In the crypt the foundations of an earlier church can be seen. It also has one of the largest organs in the world, with 6,586 pipes, on which recitals are frequently given.

In the north-west corner of the 6th, near to the Ecole des Beaux Arts, stands the building of the Institut de France, containing Academies devoted to *Belles Lettres*, Sciences, Fine Arts, Moral and Political Sciences, and the Académie Française, whose forty members meet every Thursday charged with the task of keeping the purity of the French language. It stands on a site once occupied by King Philippe le Bel, one of whose daughters-in-law had the endearing habit of discarding her lovers into the Seine once she had tired of

them, lest they spread gossip about her goings-on.

Appetites whetted by so much history and culture can be appeased at ten-thirty every morning, except Mondays, by calling in at Boudin, 6 Rue de Buci, where freshly baked *fougasses* – rich, buttery, flaky-pastry cakes from the south – are on sale. Further along, at No. 26, is a *salon de thé* belonging to Christian Constant, hailed by many as the best *patissier* in Paris.

Those with larger appetites should visit the Charcuterie Coesnon in the Rue Dauphine, off the Rue St André des Arts, which has a marvellous selection of *boudins noirs et blancs* containing a variety of fillings, as well as *terrines* and *andouillettes*.

The Rue St André des Arts was the setting for Eliot Paul's 'A Narrow Street', and where it meets the Place St Michel, so the 6th merges imperceptibly with the 5th.

... and if at the end of the day you feel worn out by it all, you can always go back to the Luxembourg Gardens and find yourself an empty bench. In Paris, no one will come along and ask you to move: at least not until closing-time, when a gendarme will appear with his whistle at the ready.

41 Rue St André-des-Arts
Tel: 43.26.48.23
Cards: DC, VISA
Closed: Saturday, Sunday, August
Nearest Metro: St Michel (4)
Map ref: 1

It is hard to picture the Rue St André-des-Arts, or for that matter Paris itself, without *Allard*; the restaurant, that is, not the owner, for sadly André Allard died in 1983.

For a while Madame Allard carried on at the stove in the tiny, open kitchen, dispensing her justly famous duck – served with turnips for a few weeks in the spring and with olives for the rest of the year, *escargot*, turbot with *beurre blanc*, superb *charlotte au chocolat* and raspberry gâteau; but now she has retired and the restaurant has been taken over by M. Bouchard (late of the *Brasserie l'Alsace*) who has promised that nothing will change. One can only hope that he will keep his promise, for *Allard* is an institution.

Certainly, the marble tables are the same, the waiters in their long cotton smocks remain, and the floors are still covered in sawdust. Kirs are dispensed across the traditional zinc bar, and there is *cassoulet* on Mondays. During the rest of the week there are copious helpings of veal on Tuesdays, leg of lamb and *coq au vin* on Wednesdays, *navarin* on Thursdays and beef with carrots on Fridays.

All of which, and much else besides, can be accompanied by delicious Burgundies which used to be sought out by André Allard himself, and many of which are 'family bottled'; Fleurie, Chiroubles, or his own favourite, 'Bonnes Mares', all kept in perfect condition in the cellars of what was once a coaching inn called La Halte de l'Eperon.

Everyone knows of *Allard* and so it is necessary to book several days ahead.

10 Rue Mabillon
Tel: 43.26.30.05
Cards: AE, DC, VISA
Closed: Sunday
23rd Dec. to Jan 2nd
Nearest Metro:
Mabillon (10)
St Sulpice (4)
Map ref: 2

The dog standing on the roof of *Aux Charpentiers* is no doubt supervising the arrival of other *chiens* who live in the neighbourhood and who seem to rate the restaurant quite highly, as do their owners, many of whom enjoy the supreme accolade of having their own serviettes pigeon-holed and permanently at the ready just inside the door.

The name stems from the fact that at one time the Guild of Master Carpenters and Cabinet-makers had its headquarters next door. Before becoming a Companion, apprentices were despatched to other cities across France in order to practise their craft, the final part of the course being the creation of miniature articles of furniture and architectural models, examples of which now form part of the decor of the restaurant along with old photographs and other mementos.

And what did carpenters in the making eat when they were not slaving away over their benches? Given the fact that the menu probably hasn't changed in years, the answer is mostly meat; generous helpings of salted pork with lentils, stuffed cabbage, pig's trotters, roast duck with olives, beef with basil, and other classic dishes which have stood the test of time; prepared in copper pans, the sauces made with *crème fleurette* (light cream rather than butter) and without flour and starch. You can start off with tomato or cucumber salad, *paté maison*, *escargots*, and round things off with various home-made fresh fruit tarts or *clafoutis*.

Drinks are dispensed from behind a long, old-fashioned bar with a traditional zinc counter. In keeping with the almost total lack of fish on the menu, the wine list is predominantly red. Bordeaux holds pride of place. Burgundy might not exist, although there are a few brief excursions into the Rhône Valley. You can end up with a nut liqueur from Brive-la-Gaillarde.

Unashamedly for *gourmands* rather than *gourmets*, but none the worse for that, *Aux Charpentiers* is one of those genuine old bistros one hopes will never die. If the number of full tables is anything to go by, that hardly seems likely in the foreseeable future. Like the *chiens*, locals and students recognize good value.

25 Rue de Buci
Tel: 43.54.79.34
Cards: AE, DC, EC, VISA
Closed: Open every day
Nearest Metro: St Germain-des-Prés (4)
Map ref: 3

An honest, hardworking, value-for-money bistro under the same management as *Le Muniche* in the Rue de Buci. Easier to get into at lunchtime than in the evening, when it stays open until the early hours, serving oysters, *poule au pot, confit de canard, gigot aux flageolets* and varieties of *choucroutes* to the converted who spill out on to the pavement in summer and fight to get inside during the winter. Try the red Haut-Poitou – it goes well with everything.

Le Procope. 13 Rue de l'Ancienne-Comédie. **Tel:** 43.26.99.20. **Cards:** AE, DC, VISA. **Closed:** July. **Nearest Metro:** Odéon (4, 10). **Map ref:** 4.

The oldest coffee shop in the world, founded in 1686, *Le Procope* has recently been renovated to good effect. In its heyday, Voltaire, Rousseau, Robespierre, Balzac and Napoleon used to sit near the entrance and pass comment on the other customers making their way upstairs; nowadays people are much too busy tucking into their *boeuf bourguignon* to bother. Usually full, but not overcrowded; the atmosphere, past reputation and historical associations are what most people go for.

La Closerie des Lilas. 171 Boulevard du Montparnasse. **Tel:** 43.26.70.50. **Cards:** AE, DC, VISA. **Nearest Metro:** Port-Royal (RER), Raspail (4, 6). **Map ref:** 5.

Another restaurant which thrives on its past associations, but worth visiting for the bar and its pianist. The food in the main terrace restaurant is expensive and the service sometimes less than gracious. On my last visit the waiter and the *maitre d'* were having a furious row through clenched teeth as they served the *pigeon de Bresse rôti* – the pigeon won by a short beak! There is a brasserie section which serves *plats du jour* at more sensible prices until the late hours. It depends a lot on whether or not you have a feeling of nostalgia when the name Hemingway is mentioned ... or Trotski!

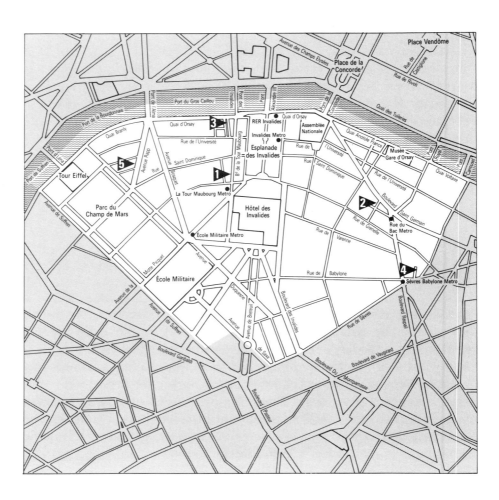

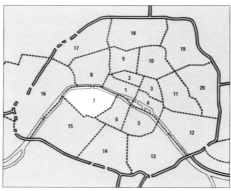

1. Chez les Anges
2. La Ferme Saint-Simon
3. Au Quai D'Orsay
4. Le Récamier
5. Sancerre

The marshal in the foreground is wasting his time pointing to the Eiffel Tower. For many people the symbol of Paris, its presence looms large in the 7th; a permanent monument to statistics. Erected in 1889 for the Paris Exhibition. Height 1042 feet. Weight 9,300 tonnes. Its 15,000 pieces held together by seven million rivets. The sway at the top on a windy day 12.7 cms – something you might not wish to know about. 45 tonnes of paint are used to refurbish it every seven years,

and each year 3,000,000 people go to see it – most of them on the day you choose, or so it feels. The view from the top makes the journey up worthwhile, but you need to love your fellow man very much to make it, and you may have lost that love forever by the time you get back down again. Rather surprisingly, there is a chic and highly regarded restaurant on the second level (the *Jules Verne*) which has its own private lift, but you will need to book well ahead. (Tel: 45.55.61.44)

Another landmark never far away is the 350 foot high dome of Les Invalides, although the lady taking her ease in the gardens of the Hôtel Biron seems to have emulated the nearby statue of Rodin's 'Thinker' and resolutely turned her back on it.

The splendidly restored eighteenth century Hôtel Biron at 77 Rue de Varenne, part of which Rodin once used as a studio, sharing it for a while with Matisse, Jean Cocteau and Isadora Duncan, now houses many of his works, together with his personal collection of furniture and art. It is open to the public from 1 May until 30 September (free on Wednesdays) and an added bonus in its leafy, slightly unkempt gardens, are the many roses which bloom in the summer months alongside 'The Thinker', 'The Burghers of Calais' and other masterpieces. If you arrive via the Varenne Metro station look out for a life-size reproduction of his sculpture of Balzac.

Les Invalides was originally built in the reign of Louis XIV to house wounded soldiers – hence the name – and at one time was home to over six thousand men. Over the years it gradually came to be used for other purposes, although always to do with the military. The

Artillery Museum was opened in 1870, followed by the Army Museum in 1896. In 1898 it saw the opening of the offices of the Military Government in Paris.

The Hôtel des Invalides occupies over thirty acres and the imposing main building is separated from the landscaped esplanade surrounding it by suitably impressive fortifications, including a moat and a large number of ancient and much photographed cannon. Everything about Les Invalides is on a grand scale. The organ in 'The Soldiers' Church' has 4,800 pipes, and the 'Dome Church' is considered by many to be the finest built since the Renaissance, as befits the final resting-place of France's most powerful Emperor.

If you have any interest at all in the events leading up to the Second World War and the war itself, the Army Museum (entrance in Boulevard de la Tour-Maubourg) is well worth a visit. Everything that possibly relates to it is on display, and there is a fascinating and often moving section devoted to the Resistance.

Everything that one says about Les Invalides also applies to the 7th arrondissement itself. For a long time the Pont Royal, again built at the request of Louis XIV, was the only bridge to cross the Seine west of the Pont Neuf, and the area became fashionable and flourished accordingly.

True, many of the buildings are now occupied by large corporations or government departments, but it remains a very dignified part of Paris. Here and there, if you are lucky, you catch a glimpse through large open doors into courtyards beyond, and it is easy to feel that, for some, life hasn't changed a great deal since the beginning of the century. Here, perhaps more than anywhere else, you know too that as a casual visitor you will never get more than that passing glimpse, for it is a very private world. Even the Boulevard Saint Germain, which further along in the 6th becomes bustling and full of student life, is here somehow more formal.

The *quais* which form the northern boundary of the 7th have become a race track, wide enough to make crossing them a hazardous not to say time-consuming occupation. However, there is now a very good reason for remaining on the south side of the river. The conversion of the old Gare d'Orsay into the Musée d'Orsay is the biggest and grandest cultural project since the Pompidou Centre was built. Devoted to the nineteenth century, it houses under one roof everything of note in the world of French art from the end of Louis Philippe's reign in 1848 to the outbreak of the first World War in 1914, including the magnificent collection of Impressionist paintings which used to be in the Jeu de Paume.

On the western side of the little park outside Sèvres Babylone Metro station there is another monument to a bygone age; Au Bon Marché. It is the most civilized of department stores; busy without ever seeming too crowded, patronized by nuns and well-to-do local housewives, it is good for oriental rugs, books, hardware, groceries, stationery, kitchen accessories, and even exotic ladies' underwear.

54 Boulevard Latour-
Maubourg
Tel: 47.05.89.86
Cards: AE, DC, EC,
VISA
Closed: Sunday evening,
Monday, 8–31 August
Nearest Metro: Latour-
Maubourg (8)
Map ref: 1

Chez les Anges acquired its name at a time when a play with a similar name was all the rage in Paris. And if the original owner, Armand Monassier, has long since retired to tend his vines, Madame Françoise Benoist still gives you a suitably angelic welcome as she ushers you into the flower-decked dining-room; itself something of an eye-opener to anyone brought up in the cloistered belief that only the English like flowers; some French restaurants must spend a fortune on them.

The cuisine embraces both classical and *nouvelle*, the former perhaps more successfully; dishes like ham with parsley and calves' liver with *pommes dauphinois* have been 'standards' for years. Although it is Burgundian and therefore puts the emphasis on meat, the fish shouldn't be ignored. The grilled *rougets*, for example, are simple, unadorned and delicious. Lobster in one form or another is usually on the menu, and occasionally they have *moules de bouchot* – mussels which cling to a pile driven into the sea bed and are smaller than usual, but twice as tasty as the big ones.

There is a large and comprehensive wine list, the dining-room is spacious with tables sufficiently wide apart to ensure reasonable privacy, and the service is swift and efficient. Madame Benoist herself takes the orders, while keeping an eagle and highly professional eye on all that is happening around her. Nothing escapes her notice, and nothing is too much trouble – you even get the bill when you ask for it, which is more than can be said of many restaurants. There is a good cheese board and a large trolley laden with classic mouth-watering fruit tarts to round things off.

Chez les Anges is slightly expensive for what is, after all, an up-market bistro. Lady guests don't get a priced menu – which could be bad news if they happen to like lobster, so by English standards it is more of a place to visit for a treat than to keep body and soul together, but that doesn't stop it being full of locals when it comes to Sunday lunchtime. It's easy to see why it is closed on Sunday evenings!

6 Rue Saint-Simon
Tel: 45.48.35.74
Cards: VISA
Closed: Saturday lunch,
Sunday, First two weeks
in August
Nearest Metro: Rue du
Bac (12)
Map ref: 2

All too often *nouvelle cuisine* – at its worst – is adventure for adventure's sake. At *La Ferme Saint-Simon*, Patrick Buret, who has worked with Lenôtre, Bocuse and Haeberlin, knows exactly what he is doing and, more important – why.

It is a sign of the quality of the cooking that although one might say, to put it kindly, 'best use has been made of the space available' in a restaurant that is always very full, one is unaware of it, savouring each new dish as it arrives. In fact, the cuisine is an admirable mixture of *nouvelle* and classical, combining the presentation and attention to detail of the former with the best of the latter.

Bavarois of mussels with tarragon, stuffed *feuilleté* of sea trout, *fricassée* of calf's kidneys and sweetbreads with juniper berries, and rabbit with *mirabelles* are standard dishes on a menu which is complemented each day by one or two additions depending on what is available in the market. *Michelin* lists 'desserts' among the recommended dishes which gained Monsieur Buret his star, and rightly so.

At lunchtime there is a fixed-price menu including wine. In the evening it is *à la carte* only. On the back of the menu there is a short list of a dozen or so minor wines recommended by the owner – all very drinkable, but a longer list is available on request.

The smiles when you arrive tend to be somewhat fixed, perhaps because they have to be switched on and off in rapid succession, and the wine waiter could do with being taken down a *cru* or two, but the rest of the staff are very amiable.

49 Quai d'Orsay
Tel: 45.51.58.58
Cards: AE, DC, EC, VISA
Closed: Sunday, August
Nearest Metro: Invalides (8, 13, RER)
Map ref: 3

If you like edible fungi, this is the place to go; Monsieur Bigeard, the chef-patron is a specialist. *Cèpes, chanterelles, girolles,* saffron milk-caps, and many others are served in a variety of different ways; with cream as a first course, with *lapin* as a main course – you name it.

But if you happen not to like mushrooms, don't be put off. There are many other delights on the menu; *pissenlit* salad (dandelion leaves with fresh tuna), beef with shallots, roast duckling, and rack of lamb. On the whole, meat is probably a better bet than fish, but the menu is very seasonal and so it is hard to be specific. Portions are vast, but half portions of most dishes may be ordered, which is sensible.

Au Quai d'Orsay is a very Parisian restaurant, usually crowded with hearty Parisian eaters whose every need is quickly attended to by bustling waitresses who understand what eating on a grand scale is all about. It is certainly not the sort of place to go to if you are on a diet or want a quiet, lingering meal. There are some reasonably priced wines on the list. You will certainly need to reserve.

Monsieur Bigeard has recently opened the *Annexe du Quai* in the adjoining Rue Surcouf; a smaller bistro with an all-inclusive menu of traditional specialities. Closed: Saturday, Sunday. Tel: 45.51.48.48.

4 Rue Récamier
Tel: 45.48.86.58
Cards: DC, EC
Closed: Sunday
Nearest Metro: Sèvres-Babylone (10–12)
Map ref: 4

Much patronized by writers and editors, *Le Récamier* is a restaurant to which one finds oneself returning again and again, assured of a warm welcome, deliciously fruity Kirs, exceptionally good wines from Burgundy and the Côtes du Rhone, and a menu which revolves around such classic dishes as *oeufs en meurette, boeuf bourguignon* – served with *tagliatelle*, lobster *à la Nage*, and *rognons de veau au Santenay*, followed by strawberry ice or *tarte aux pommes*. The ingredients are as fresh as it is possible for them to be, arriving every morning from Monsieur Cantegrit's own farm.

Situated in a quiet, dead-end street off the busy Rue de Sèvres, *Le Récamier* is of the district and yet set apart. In the summer months, when there are tables outside amongst the potted plants, knowledgeable gourmet sparrows possessed of *le courage* arrive on your table to share the bread – or even take it away if they are given half a chance.

It is a regional restaurant, from an area of France which doesn't believe in letting customers go away feeling hungry, and if you have a deep enough pocket the wine list is full of temptations to aid your digestion.

Sancerre. 22 Avenue Rapp. **Tel:** 45.51.75.91. **Closed:** Saturday evening, Sunday. **Nearest Metro:** Ecole Militaire (8). **Map ref:** 5.

A small bistro cum wine bar noted for its Sancerre wine, its *Crottin de Chavignol* goat cheese, its smoked ham and its *andouillette*. A useful address if you are in the area. Popular with people who work at the nearby Cognac-Jay television studios, so you need to get there early.

8ᵉ ARRONDISSEMENT

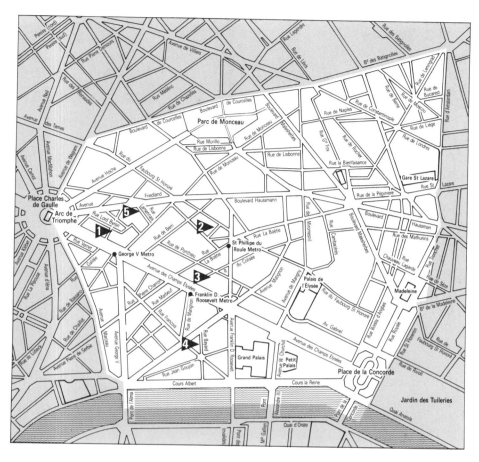

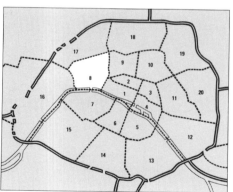

1. Le Lord Gourmand
2. La Poularde Landaise
3. La Boutique à Sandwiches
4. Savy
5. Taillevant

Broad and tree-lined, the setting for innumerable military parades and state occasions, from the annual 14 July celebrations to the final lap of the Tour de France cycle race; flanked by cinemas, night-clubs, expensive pavement cafés, airline offices, car showrooms, luxury shops and arcades, gardens and fountains; bustling, noisy, synonymous with bright lights and sparkling champagne, the Avenue des Champs Elysées, arguably the most beautiful avenue in the world, acts as a magnet to the cosmopolitan crowds thronging its pavements.

The Avenue des Champs Élysées.

The very mention of its name conjures up waves of feeling for the magic that is Paris.

It is hard to believe that until the beginning of the nineteenth century the area either side of the Rond Point really was known as the 'Elysian Fields', undeveloped and deserted save for a tiny sprinkling of houses.

The crowds of people now thronging the avenue must have been as far away from the thoughts of those dwelling there as they clearly are now from the mind of this little girl living out her dreams near the marionette theatre with the aid of a stick and some gravel, completely oblivious to the never-ending roar of the traffic.

Equally lost to all but their immediate surroundings are these philatelists who gather in the Avenue de Marigny every weekend, come rain or come shine, to talk shop and to do business in Paris's largest open-air stamp market.

Elsewhere, the 8th is the Elysée Palace, home of Presidents; the ultra-smart Rue du Faubourg St Honoré, with its art galleries and *haute-couture* salons; the Place de la Madeleine with its huge, windowless church rubbing shoulders with the flower market; Fauchon, where the smell of baking tarts draws the crowds and where everything in the way of luxury foodstuffs can be bought at a price; and that most civilized of department stores, Aux Trois Quartiers;

Maxims, where one doesn't go so much for the food as for its memories; the Café de la Paix, where you can sit outside and watch the world go by; the Drugstore des Champs Elysées; the Grand Palais and the Petit Palais, where the great art exhibitions are held; most of the grand hotels and the great perfume houses; the Saint-Lazare area, with its railway station, the Church of St Augustin with its huge dome, and the Conservatoire National de Musique, which houses a fine collection of historical musical instruments; the Palais de la Découverte – the museum of discovery; and the Pont de l'Alma, where every half-hour during the season you can board one of the vast *Vedettes* which ply up and down the river, and where in winter passing Parisians keep a watchful eye on the statue of a French Algerian soldier in order to gauge the height of the Seine – when it's up to his shoulders it's time to leave town.

The 8th arrondissement is also the peace and relative quiet of the Parc Monceau where well-to-do mothers and uniformed nannies from rich families gather to give the occupants of their *voitures des enfants* an airing most afternoons. You would be well advised to get there early if you want a bench to yourself. Older children play in the sandpits, just as Marcel Proust did with his friend Antoinette Fauve when they were young.

The park was originally laid out in 1778 by Louis Carmontelle as a garden for Philippe-Egalité, Duke of Orleans. By all accounts it was a fabulous affair, full of flowers and follies, including pagodas, windmills and a Roman temple. A few of the follies still remain, and with its winding paths and shrubs and small lake it is a pleasant spot to be at any time of the year.

Imagine what a sensation the first parachutist must have caused in October 1797 when he jumped out of a balloon three thousand feet up and landed in the middle of it all.

9 Rue Lord Byron
Tel: 43.59.07.27
Cards: AE, VISA
Closed: Saturday, Sunday, August, One week at Christmas
Nearest Metro: George V (1)
Map ref: 1

Daniel Météry, the chef-patron, reached the Rue Lord Byron via the Troisgros Brothers in Roanne, the Hotel Windsor in Paris, and Paul Bocuse in Collonges-au-Mont-d'Or. He is a quiet, unassuming man, who only emerges from his kitchen at coffee time to enquire rather diffidently if you have enjoyed your meal. If you compliment him on the *tuille amandes* which arrive with the coffee, and which may well be the best you have every tasted, his face lights up. Ask him how he achieves such perfection and he will give a Gallic shrug and explain that for six months of his life he made them every day and threw them away until his mentors at the time were satisfied. He sees nothing remarkable in that, but it explains why you will eat deliciously well at *Le Lord Gourmand*.

Hardly more than a stone's throw away from the noise and bustle of the Champs Elysées, it is, as the saying goes, a veritable haven of peace and quiet. The dining-room is comfortably small, with well-spaced tables; the lighting soft, and the paintings on the wall above average. Busy at lunchtime, it is much quieter in the evening and an ideal *rendez-vous* for a candle-lit dinner.

Madame Météry is the perfect hostess, chic and welcoming, and the service is unobtrusively impeccable. The wine list has a good selection of clarets. Highly recommended for a first course is the *gâteau* of vegetables with tomato purée, but it would be invidious to single out things to follow; they all show the kind of imaginative touches and combinations one might expect from someone who trained with Bocuse.

Dogs are not only welcome, if they choose from the *à la carte* menu they even get a napkin laid out for them on the floor beside their owner's table (at least, that's what happened on the occasion of my last visit). There is a fixed-price menu.

You leave feeling very happy and planning your next visit.

4 Rue Saint-Philippe-du-Roule
Tel: 43.59.20.25
Cards: AE, VISA
Closed: Saturday, Sunday, Holidays
Nearest Metro: Saint-Philippe du-Roule (9)
Map ref: 2

Another restaurant which is not too far away from the Champs Elysées, and yet in the evenings in particular, one could be in another world. The interior is extremely rustic and if it ever found itself in a state of seige during a bad winter — which is much more likely to happen at lunchtime — the roaring fire could be kept going ad infinitum by judicious use of items adorning the walls.

Both contemporary design and *nouvelle cuisine* have by-passed *La Poularde Landaise* — they probably missed the turning off Rue du Faubourg-Saint-Honoré, and a good thing too. Had representatives of either entered the restaurant they would have encountered the beady eye of a large duck (stuffed) perched on top of the coat cupboard, and if they survived that then they would have been sent packing by the waitress, who would have stood none of that nonsense.

Everything about *La Poularde Landaise* is warm: the welcome, the fire, the food — especially the food, which arrives *très chaud*. On the last occasion the dish the *escargots* arrived in was so hot they kept on cooking for a good five minutes before they could be touched; somewhat to their detriment, but nothing is perfect.

As might be expected, the emphasis is on food from the Landaise region of south-west France; which means goose, bacon, aubergine, caviar — all served in generous portions at reasonable prices. Wines from the area include a very drinkable house red called Bearne, from the Domaine Brascasse Allan Brument, which goes well with the food.

More of a place for a cold winter's evening than the summer. There is a fixed-price menu which includes a Kir and 'Vins du Pays à discretion'.

La Boutique à Sandwiches. 12 Rue du Colisée. **Tel:** 43.59.56.69. **Closed:** Sunday, August. **Nearest Metro:** Franklin D. Roosevelt (1, 9). **Map ref:** 3.

A good place to go for a lunchtime snack, if 'snack' is the right word to describe *valais raclette* – a Swiss dish made up of varieties of melted cheese served with potatoes and pickled onions, which is the upper floor's speciality. On the ground floor there is vast array of sandwiches, cold meats and *plats du jour*. Popular and crowded; competition for tables is fierce, so get there early.

Savy. 23 Rue Bayard. **Tel:** 47.23.46.98. **No cards. Closed:** Sunday, August. **Nearest Metro:** Franklin D. Roosevelt (1, 9). **Map ref:** 4.

Crowded at lunchtime – the studios of Radio Luxembourg are just across the street – *Savy* is more of a place to visit in the evening, when a certain calm descends, broken only by the steady sound of clinking glasses and happy eaters chomping their way through dishes from the owner's home ground, the Auvergne: *navarin* of lamb, stuffed cabbage, knuckle of ham with lentils, *blanquette* of veal – each day has its specialities, all of which are helped on their way by the house Cahors, which also goes well with the regional cheeses. There is also some fine old Armagnac which is a fitting accompaniment to the *tarte aux prunes*.

Taillevent. 15 Rue Lamennais. **Tel:** 45.63.39.94. **Closed:** Saturday, Sunday, August, 8–16 February. **Nearest Metro:** George V (1). **Map ref:** 5.

You will need to telephone several weeks in advance if you want to reserve a table at *Taillevent*, and even then you may well fall foul of the unofficial quota system operated by many of the top Paris restaurants in order to limit the number of foreign visitors. If you are a large dog you will never get in.

In many ways it is a contradiction in terms to include *Taillevent* amongst the 'others', since to most people it is the top restaurant in Paris, and therefore in a class of its own. Everything one could possibly say about it has already been said many times over, so it is pointless repeating it. On the other hand, one couldn't leave it out. Anyone at all interested in food should go there at least once, for Monsieur Jean-Claude Vrinat and his staff are dedicated to quality and perfection in all its aspects, and the food can be accompanied by wine from a list which must be the best in Paris and is certainly not over-priced.

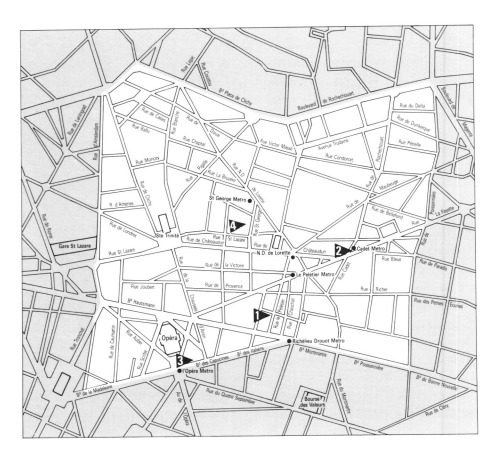

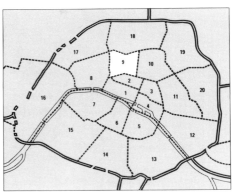

1. Au Petit Riche
2. Les Trois Portes
3. Le Grand Café
4. Ty-Coz

The 9th is an arrondissement of contrasts, both culturally and architecturally; from the Opéra to the Folies-Bergère. At one end of the scale architecturally is the Hôtel Drouot, Paris's premier auction rooms where every year in its sixteen rooms some 600,000 objects from stamps to rare items of furniture fall under the auctioneers' ivory hammers.

Everything is extremely well organized. Objects are displayed in the sale room on the day prior to the auction and there will be someone on hand to give you an estimate of prices likely to be fetched

The Hôtel Drouot – Paris's premier auction house.

if something catches your fancy. Payment can be by cash (if you want to take it away the same day) or by cheque, plus a sliding scale of charges ranging from around 17% for the lower priced objects, to 10%. There is a thirty-year legally binding guarantee of authenticity on anything you buy. But non-buying visitors are welcome, and, like the Law Courts, the Hôtel Drouot provides an absorbing theatrical experience.

In striking contrast to the Hôtel Drouot is the area north of the Rue de Châteaudun and bounded roughly by the Rue Notre-Dame-de-Lorette to the east, Rue d'Amsterdam to the west, and Rue Chaptel to the north. Nowadays it is a somewhat neglected part of

Paris, but in its heyday at the beginning of the nineteenth century, when it was known as 'New Athens', it was for a time the centre of literary and artistic life. Georges Sand, Liszt, Chopin, Delacroix, Ingres, Millet, Cabanel, Gustave Moreau, Alexandre Dumas the elder and others entertained each other, not in the cafés of the Boulevard Montmartre, but in elegant houses such as this at 16 Rue Chaptal; once the home of Ary Scheffer, now the Renan-Scheffer Museum.

It is a rewarding area in which to take a quiet stroll – and one which is full of surprises.

Most of the life of the 9th arrondissement takes place north of a line running along the Boulevards Capucines, Italiens, Montmartre and Poissonnière.

Paris's greatest monument to the Second Empire majestically overlooks the point where the Boulevard Capucines crosses the Place de l'Opéra. Debussy likened the outside of it to a railway station and the inside to a Turkish Bath. Be that as it may, the Paris Opera House has a permanent company of 1100 – half the total audience capacity, and is the largest theatre in the world, with a stage capable of accommodating 450 players. Haussman demolished an entire *quartier* to provide space for it, and then built the Avenue de l'Opéra to give the whole a suitably grand approach.

No Turkish Bath can ever have boasted such a magnificent staircase, or a chandelier weighing sixteen tons. These, and the ceiling painted by Chagall, can be viewed as part of a guided tour every weekday. Tickets for performances go on sale at the box office fourteen days beforehand, but there is always a great demand and most have already been sold by subscription anyway.

Behind the Opera House is the Boulevard Haussman, home for two of Paris's largest department stores, Galeries Lafayette and Au Printemps. Between them they cater for practically anything and everything you might require and are so vast – both are a series of interconnected buildings – that you can either want to spend a whole day in them or to come out again after five minutes. If you belong to the former category and start to flag around lunchtime, the cafeteria at the Galeries Lafayette is above average and looks out on to the Opera House.

The 9th arrondissement also boasts a number of thriving *passages*. As with those in the 2nd arrondissement, they recall the days of the *Grands Boulevards* and have lately been enjoying a new lease of life. The passage du Havre, near Gare St-Lazare, with entrances at 69 Rue Caumartin and 109 Rue St-Lazare, is the most popular and there is a haven for model train enthusiasts at the 'Maison des Trains'.

The Passage Jouffrey, at 10 Boulevard Montmartre, houses the Grevin wax-works museum, where the famous are behind glass and politicians have a habit of biting the dust within seconds of being deposed. Halfway along is the Hôtel Chopin, the façade of which is classified as a National Monument. The rooms are small, but it is exceptionally quiet in an area which is normally very noisy. There is also a lovely toy shop, Pain d'Epices, full of things which evoke memories of one's own childhood, many of which are created by the owners in their workshop. Fine for doll's house furniture, bric-a-brac and things made out of the wood or sheet metal.

Across the Rue de la Grange-Batelière at the other end of the Passage Jouffrey is the Passage Verdeau, which provides a happy hunting ground for lovers of old books, particularly strip cartoons and science fiction; old gramophone records and, at the Magasin

Verdeau, vintage cameras dating back to before the turn of the century. The far end of the Passage Verdeau brings you out into an area of small food shops, street markets and, to the right of the Rue Richer, the Folies-Bergère, now sadly living on past memories, but still offering a night out which is peculiarly and spectacularly its own.

Nearby, at 35 Rue du Faubourg Montmartre, stands La Mère de Famille, looking for all the world like a child's toy sweetshop come to

life. Established in 1791, its windows are packed with mouth-watering goodies: boxes of bon-bons, jars of boiled sweets, trays of chocolates, tins of biscuits and seasonable offerings of home-made *confitures* and honey from all over France. You enter at your peril. As one might expect, it opens at seven-thirty in the morning to catch the trade of those on their way to school, and is sensibly closed during the month of August and the first week in September.

25 Rue le Peletier
Tel: 47.70.68.68
Cards: AE, VISA
Closed: Sunday, August
Nearest Metro: Le
Peletier (7), Richelieu
Drouot (8, 9)
Map ref: 1

In an area where good restaurants are surprisingly thin on the ground, *Au Petit Riche* merits a visit because it is the kind of establishment French people take for granted, expecting to eat as well as their forefathers will have done over the last hundred years and not being disappointed. The food is sound, without ever reaching heights to which it doesn't aspire anyway.

You dine in a series of rooms linked by corridors and kitchens, each room holding twenty or so people. The décor is wood, painted ceilings, mirrors and red upholstery. The windows are frosted glass etched with imitation curtains. Overhead there are brass luggage racks, so that the overall effect is not unlike that of sitting in an oversize railway carriage, and it wouldn't be too surprising if one day it steamed off up the Boulevard Haussman.

At lunchtime it is packed with journalists and businessmen tucking in to ham from Meursault, *andouillette vouvrillone*, and hot apple tart fresh from the oven. Other specialities worth considering are: *terrine de haddock au coulis de tomates* and *sauté de veau aux poireaux*.

The emphasis is on the Loire region, and on the back of the menu there is a good list of sound and reasonably priced wines from that area, including a red Sancerre. The Kirs are fruity.

In the evening it is again well patronized by the French – always a good sign, but many other accents can be heard from those venturing out from nearby hotels in the *Grands Boulevards*.

65 Rue La Fayette
Tel: 48.78.23.04
Cards: AE, DC, VISA
Closed: Saturday (lunch)
August
Nearest Metro: Cadet
(7)
Map ref: 2

If it is your first evening in Paris for a while and you want to re-establish contact with the French way of life, particularly if it happens to be Sunday evening when many restaurants are closed, then *Les Trois Portes* is the place to go.

It is yet another of those bistros which could have been there for ever (in fact, it first opened in 1840), and one feels the décor has survived renovation over the years and probably hasn't changed greatly since the Bel family took over in the early twenties.

Two of the 'three doors' open on to the Rue La Fayette and the Rue Cadet respectively, whilst the third is only a few steps away from the Metro – a big bonus if you don't like to walk far after a meal.

The food is all that one might expect; that is to say, *terrines*, steak with *pommes frites*, sea-food platters and various dishes of the day are all totally reliable and professionally cooked and served.

It is a 'ticket restaurant', so inevitably there are tourists from nearby hotels 'sans restaurant', but it is a case of first come first served with the tables and no favouritism is shown to the many French people who also patronize it. The only thing to watch out for when it comes to nearing the end of the meal is that you get a 'French' menu and not one in either English or German, both of which mysteriously lack certain items, like *fromage blanc*.

It is the kind of place where a woman, or for that matter a man, can happily dine alone, although if you are a man you have the added bonus of being able to dwell on the statistical possibility of sitting next to a beautiful girl, resplendent in diamonds, who gives you a mysterious handshake as she leaves, for during the week it is much patronized by artists from the Folies-Bergère, members of the Diamond Merchants Club, and a local branch of the Masonic Lodge.

The current Monsieur Bel is ever-present, taking orders, making sure everyone is happy and their needs are being properly attended to.

4 Boulevard des
Capucines
Tel: 47.42.75.77
Cards: AE, DC, VISA
Closed: Never
Nearest Metro: Opéra
(3, 7, 8)
Map ref: 3

If *Au Petit Riche* can be likened to a railway carriage, then *Le Grand Café* is an ocean liner. Like its sister ships, *L'Alsace* in the Champs-Elysées, and the *Pied de Cochon* in Les Halles, it never closes, but carries on, lights blazing, full steam ahead, day and night, all through the year. Unsinkable. Unstoppable.

Everything about it represents a different way of life. The décor harks back to the days of the *Grands Boulevards*, there is always a vast quantity of shellfish on refrigerated display, and even the waiters – professional to their fingertips – seem to have been chosen so that their moustaches match their black evening dress.

And the food? The shellfish speaks for itself, and as *Le Grand Café* is part of the Blanc Empire, which also owns Boucherie Blanc, the quality of the meat is guaranteed. Popular with French people and surprisingly untouristy in an area where they are fairly thick on the ground, *Le Grand Café* is best on classically plain dishes, all of which can be accompanied by wine from an exceptionally good list.

The 'Indian Room' is where the first ever moving film is reputed to have been shown.

Ty-Coz. 35 Rue St-Georges. **Tel:** 48.78.42.95. **Cards:** AE, DC, VISA. **Closed:** Sunday, Monday, 11–17 August. **Nearest Metro:** St Georges (12). **Map ref:** 4.

A Breton restaurant specializing almost exclusively in fish; grilled bass, *lotte* with cider, turbot with *beurre nantais*, *cotriade* (a Breton version of *bouillabaisse*) – if there are at least four of you and it is ordered in advance – not to mention fresh oysters, prawns and crabs. The menu is written on a slate, there are *crêpes* for dessert, and through it all you can drink Marquis de Goulaine muscadet or Breton cider.

Madame Libois' daughter runs an identical *Ty-Coz* at No. 333 Rue de Vaugirard in the 15th arrondissement. Tel: 48.28.42.69. Nearest Metro: Convention (12).

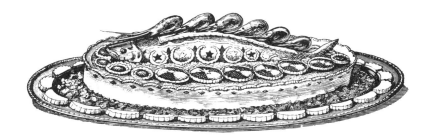

10ᵉ ARRONDISSEMENT

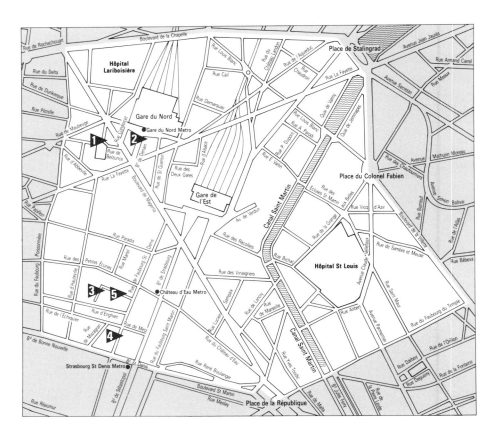

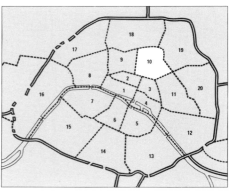

1. Chez Michel
2. Terminus Nord
3. Brasserie Flo
4. Julien
5. Le Paillon

The 10th arrondissement remains an unfashionable area of Paris and because of this it is largely unspoilt. The nearest it came to disaster in recent years was when the late President Pompidou devised a grand scheme to fill in the Canal St Martin, which bisects it on the eastern side, and build an autoroute in its place. Luckily the public outcry was such that the idea was abandoned. It would have been a great shame had it gone through, for this is Simenon country, off the main tourist tracks, full of small workshops, and with many literary and filmic associations, providing the setting for Marcel Carné's *Hôtel du Nord* and *Quai des Brumes*, to name but two.

Bath-house at number 198 Rue Lafayette.

The tree-lined canal was built by Napoleon I to provide a link between Paris and the French and Belgian waterways of the North. The idea came from no less a person than Leonardo da Vinci, who also invented the canal lock which made it possible.

Between La Villette and the Seine there is a drop of some eighty feet via nine locks. It is an atmospheric world full of delightful examples of early engineering; iron footbridges, swing-bridges and vaulted tunnels, which can best be seen by taking the three-hour-long catamaran trip which runs daily during the summer months (see 19th arrondissement).

However, if you are exploring the area on foot and happen to be a film buff to boot, it is worth making a small detour at the northern end of the canal to No. 198 Rue Lafayette, where the Bains Lafayette,

The smallest house in Paris.

the bathing establishment immortalized in perhaps the greatest of all French films, *Les Enfants du Paradis*, still stands.

The southern extremity of the 10th is marked by part of the *Grands Boulevards*, the Boulevard Bonne Nouvelle and the Boulevard St Denis. Like the *Périphérique*, they were built on the site of former fortifications and enjoyed a period of being fashionable, but sadly this is no longer so. Only Portes St Denis and St Martin serve as a reminder of better days.

A little further north, in Rue du Château d'Eau, is the smallest house in Paris – just three feet wide and fifteen feet high, although putting its number sideways on above the door does seem to be rubbing it in a bit.

North again there is an area of china and glass emporia in and around Rue de Paradis. Most of those in the Rue de Paradis itself are expensive and more for window gazing, although Baccarat at No.

30 *bis* does have a museum of glassware next door (closed weekends and holidays). However, if you are interested in everyday china, the Création della Torre in Rue Martel is well worth a visit. It is the least conspicuous of the establishments, but it is the cheapest and the most rewarding; a happy hunting ground for Christmas presents. You enter a courtyard at No. 12 and then make your way into a rather forbidding building on your right. Behind an unmarked door immediately ahead of you is an Aladdin's cave of everything for the kitchen in white china. In other rooms there are decorated pots, vases and apothecaries' jars in profusion.

Also in Rue de Paradis, at No. 18, on the site of an old Boulenger ceramics warehouse, is the Musée de l'Affiche. Entry is through a small courtyard decorated with pictorial tiles and inside there is a collection of over 50,000 old posters, including works by Toulouse-Lautrec and many other famous nineteenth and turn-of-the-century artists. There is a programme of continuously changing exhibitions, so that over a period of time all the posters go on display. The museum, which is open every afternoon except Mondays, Tuesdays and holidays, also houses a large collection of early film posters.

The north-eastern part of the 10th is mostly given over to the railways – the Gare du Nord and the Gare de l'Est, and as in most cities where there are large railway termini, whole areas remain isolated, cut off from contact with each other by deep cuttings and acres of rails, and so remain unfashionable. For some reason, railway stations often seem to attract the worst in mankind. Perhaps it's the thought of all the lost travellers with their luggage, not knowing quite where to go. Stations serving the north always seem marginally worse, and Paris is no exception. The area around the Gare du Nord is largely populated by cheap hotels, North African trinket sellers crouching for hours on end over rugs, and touts for practically anything you might require.

So it is to the canal, with its echoes of Simenon, that one inevitably returns. Here and there are little cafés where you can picture Maigret, pipe in mouth, beginning one of his investigations; ignoring the glances from the locals while he stands at the bar and orders the first of many drinks to come.

On the canal itself there are other reminders as huge barges from Belgium glide past, all neat and ship-shape, a bicycle, sometimes even a car stowed on deck, and nowadays the inevitable television aerial. As they draw near they afford tantalizing glimpses of check table cloths and polished brass behind lace curtains, and invoke a momentary feeling of restlessness and envy that other people's lives can be so orderly and problem free, yet contained in so small a space. Then they are gone.

Architecturally, apart from the stations themselves, there is little in the way of buildings of historical interest in the northern half of the 10th, still less anything even remotely connected with any kind of culture.

The canal St Martin, where lovers stroll and old ladies pause to

drink in the sunshine while on their way to do the daily shopping.

ICI EST TOMBÉ
LE 20 AOÛT 1944
ANDRÉ CHENNEVIÉRE
POÈTE ET JOURNALISTE
MORT POUR LA LIBERTÉ

But all you need for a game of Boules is a level area of ground and you're in business. Not a cochonet's throw from the Gare de l'Est is one such little area ...

... and nearby, let into a wall, is one of those sad reminders one comes across all too often in Paris and other parts of France, that these things are worth fighting and, if necessary, dying for.

10 Rue de Belzunce
Tel: 48.78.44.14
Cards: AE, DC, VISA
Closed: Friday, Saturday, August
Nearest Metro: Gare du Nord (4, 5)
Map ref: 1

Tucked away in a side street not far from the Gare du Nord and close to the church of St Vincent, *Chez Michel* is a good, solid two-star *Michelin* restaurant for the gourmand as well as the gourmet. It is relatively small and well patronized by regulars, so it is usually necessary to book, especially on a Sunday.

Monsieur Michel Tounissoux himself is much in evidence; taking orders with approving nods or advising when he thinks it is necessary, greeting new arrivals, going off to supervise the cooking, returning later to make sure you are enjoying the result.

The food is more classical than *nouvelle*, although in recent years there have been signs of it hovering somewhere in between; a concession to changing fashions and tastes, as Monsieur Tounissoux experiments with lighter sauces and more exotic combinations of ingredients. Specialities are *salade gourmande, coquilles St Jacques, omelette Président Vincent Bourrel* and *crêpes au Grand Marnier*, all cooked to perfection.

There is a good wine list with a formidable range of old Armagnacs to prepare you for the bill, which won't be small, but by then you will be past caring anyway.

23 Rue Dunkerque
Tel: 42.85.05.15
Cards: AE, DC, VISA
Open: Every day until
12.30
Nearest Metro: Gare
du Nord (4, 5)
Map ref: 2

Terminus Nord is the second of the group of restaurants owned by Jean-Paul Bucher, three of which are in this arrondissement, and all that has been said about *Le Vaudeville* in the 2nd applies. But it's worth saying again, for in all of them you get excellent value for money. The food is first class and intelligently prepared; the wine well chosen. This means it is necessary to book at peak times and, what is even more important, arrive on time, for tables are not allowed to remain empty for long. The setting is Belle Epoque and the menu concentrates on sea-food.

Brasserie Flo. 6 Cour des Petites-Ecuries. **Tel:** 47.70.13.59. **Cards:** AE, DC, VISA. **Closed:** 1–28 August. **Nearest Metro:** Château d'Eau (4). **Map ref:** 3.

The first restaurant in the Bucher empire, specializing in Alsatian food in a genuine 1900s setting. If you need a sobering thought while you quaff beer drawn from the wood or house wine served in a pitcher, reflect on the fact that when Monsieur Bucher opened it in the early seventies he had only one customer. Today the four restaurants between them serve over 3,000 customers a day and employ a staff of 450.

Julien. 16 Rue du Faubourg St Denis. **Tel:** 47.70.12.06. **Cards:** AE, DC, VISA. **Closed:** 1–28 July. **Nearest Metro:** Strasbourg St Denis (4, 8, 9). **Map ref:** 4.

1890s décor enlived by a collection of genuine Art Nouveau designs; clientele to match – mostly advertising and show business people.

Le Paillon. 4 Cour des Petites-Ecuries. **Tel:** 45.23.02.77. **Cards:** VISA. **Closed:** Sunday, Monday, August. **Nearest Metro:** Château d'Eau (4). **Map ref:** 5.

A charming little restaurant in the same court as *Brasserie Flo*. Roger Roux, the chef-patron, specializes in Provençal cooking; stuffed vegetables, *aioli garni*, etc., with wines to match the appropriately sunny welcome. The tables are fairly close together and each has its own little decorated vase of artificial flowers, a number of which appear to have been dead-headed at some point in time – perhaps by waiting customers, for speed and efficiency is not the name of the game and Monsieur Roux, who wears clogs, enjoys a chat.

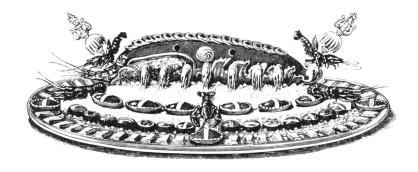

11ᵉ ARRONDISSEMENT

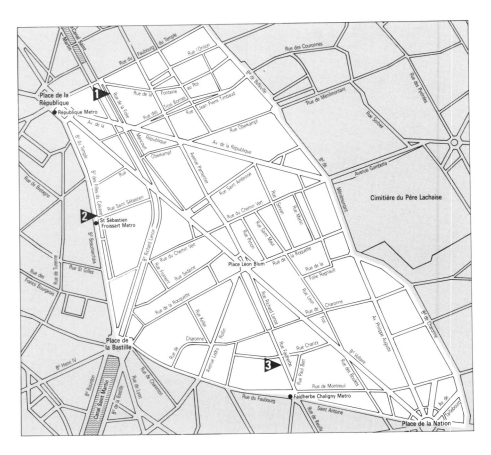

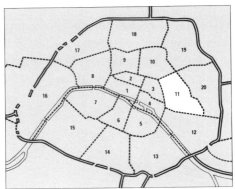

1. Auberge Pyrénées Cévennes
2. Le Repaire de Cartouche
3. A Sousceyrac

At first sight, if it wasn't for a corner of the Place de la République in the north, a segment of the Place de la Nation in the south-east and a quarter of Baron Haussman's answer to insurrection, the vast Place de la Bastille in the south-western corner, there would be no great reason for visiting the 11th arrondissement. Even the Canal St Martin goes underground at the Rue du Faubourg-du-Temple and doesn't surface again until it is safely past the Place de la Bastille.

Until the seventeenth century the area east of the Bastille was outside the city walls and many craftsmen fled Paris to escape the

Cleaning time for the canal St Martin.

strict rules laid down by their guilds. They sought refuge in a convent in the village of Saint Antoine and made it their home. Consequently, the district between the Faubourg Saint-Antoine and the Rue de Charonne is almost entirely given over to their descendants, most of whom specialize in the making of furniture and associated fittings.

Practically every small street and alley-way has its quota of work-shops. Elsewhere in the arrondissement other workshops specialize in metalwork and precision engineering.

Near the Place de la Bastille there is also a strong Auvergnaise influence with its own tradition and way of life. In the old days the Rue du Lappe was considered *the* place for dancing the *musette* – a French version of dancing to the sound of bagpipes in the Scottish style – hence the *bals musettes*. In time bagpipes gave way to the accordion, *apaches* and their girlfriends moved in and a whole new folk-lore concerning the Paris underworld was born. Most of the old *bals* have disappeared, although a few survive and the population remains unchanged, as can be seen by the glimpses of smoked hams and sausages hanging from the ceiling of cafés and restaurants.

The inhabitants of the 11th keep themselves very much to themselves, and despite its historical background, there are few buildings of interest remaining.

The Petite Roquette prison has been pulled down and replaced by an apartment block. First used as a kind of transit camp for prisoners awaiting transport to even less happy places, it was named after a wild flower which used to grow in the waste-lands surrounding it. Mention is made in some guide-books of five black stones set in the roadway outside where the main entrance used to be in the Rue de la Roquette, to mark where the guillotine was erected, but even those seem to have disappeared.

At the eastern end of Rue de la Roquette is the 20th arrondissement and the Père Lachaise cemetery. If you plan to visit the grave of Edith Piaf, then you might like to make a short detour first to No. 5 Rue Crespin du Gast and the Musée Edith Piaf (not far from the Menilmontant Metro station). The museum is quite small – only two rooms on the fourth floor of an old apartment block, but it contains lots of interesting mementoes of her life: clothes, photographs, paintings, some surprising letters to wives of various lovers, and a couch which could probably tell a few stories.

Reputedly born in the early hours of 19 December 1915, on the steps of No. 72 Rue de Belleville (although her birth certificate gives the address as 4 Rue de la Chine), daughter of an intinerant Italian street-singer mother and a circus acrobat father from Normandy, blind at the age of eight, able to see again at thirteen following a pilgrimage to Lisieux, brought up by her grandmother until she was fourteen, when she and her father took to the pavements again entertaining passers-by, she was aptly nicknamed 'Piaf' – Paris argot for 'sparrow' – by the locals. And despite her international fame, that is what she remained – a little sparrow who craved love and in her songs shared that craving with millions of others, so it is fitting that the museum should be in a part of Paris which remained so very much with her all through her life. Visits are by appointment only – ring 43.55.52.72 – and while you are there the caretaker sets the scene by playing records of that haunting voice.

106 Rue de la Folie-Méricourt
Tel: 43.57.33.78
Cards: None
Closed: Saturday, Sunday, August
Nearest Metro: République (3, 5, 8, 9, 11)
Map ref: 1

The slightly confusing mixture of names reflects the arrival of a 'new' owner – Monsieur Philippe Serbource – some years ago, but having said that, *nouvelle* is not the first word which springs to mind when you enter the *Auberge Pyrénéees Cévennes/Chez Philippe*; either with regard to the décor or to the food which follows.

Tucked away in a side street across the Canal St Martin from the Place de la République, it is patronized by solid local trenchermen of the old school, plus a sprinkling of trenchermen's wives. As soon as you sit down you are offered a Kir as a matter of course along with the menu which, like the old wooden sabots, shields and posters of bull fights on the stone walls, reflects the Basque origins.

Monsieur Serbouce does all the shopping for the food and the ordering of the wine, and he likes his guests to eat well. But be warned: portions are large, so don't yield to temptation or the blandishments of the patron and order *piperade* (a form of omelette with ham, onions, peppers and tomatoes) for a first course, followed by *cassoulet* – another speciality. Separately, each is more than enough for one meal; together they could prove fatal. Other specialities are *foie gras* – prepared on the premises, and *cochonnailles de pays* – sausages which come in a large basket so that you can help yourself.

The wine list contains some good clarets and Burgundies, but is also interesting for its selection of smaller, local wines which one wouldn't find elsewhere.

8 Boulevard des Filles-
du-Calvaire
Tel: 47.00.25.86
Cards: VISA
Closed: Saturday,
Sunday, 17 July–
15 August, holidays
Nearest Metro: St
Sébastien Froissart (8)
Map ref: 2

As with *Le Trou Gascon* in the neighbouring 12th, we are in 'Three Musketeers' country. Most of the waiters sport suitably large moustaches, but none quite so magnificent as that belonging to the owner, Raymond Pocous, a one-time printer turned restaurateur.

Monsieur Pocous takes charge the moment you enter, and delights in discussing not only the food, but all that goes with it; from the house apéritif, through the wine list, to the choice of Armagnac at the end of the meal. He is not only an enthusiastic host, but a generous and endearingly honest one as well. On the first visit, whilst approving my choice of what was a fairly expensive Chassagne Montrachet, and certainly not decrying it, he strongly recommended a Pouilly Fumé at half the price as being a more suitable accompaniment to the dish we had ordered. And when it came to making a choice at the end from an array of some forty or so bas-Armagnacs, generous helpings of several alternatives were presented for my delectation beforehand.

As for the food, it is naturally from the south-west corner of France, but the chef, Raphael Pouchois, manages to avoid the heartiness one sometimes encounters. *Confits* of duck and goose, *quenelles* of wild salmon, *foie gras* and Chalosse beef figure on a menu which also has a good selection of desserts of which another speciality of the region, *la tourtière Landaise à l'Armagnac*, can be recommended.

The décor, which is provincial wood, goes with the moustaches.

If you happen to visit *Le Repaire de Cartouche* at lunchtime, then it is worth allowing time either beforehand or afterwards to explore the surrounding area, which is full of specialist shops; everything from old-fashioned corset makers to camera repairers (if you want to see the complete works of a Leica stripped down, look in the window of La Maison du Leica at No. 54) and the wonderful Rougier et Plé, purveyors of artists' materials and model-making equipment, at 13–15 Boulevard des Filles-du-Calvaire.

35 Rue Faidherbe
Tel: 43.71.65.30
Cards: AE, VISA
Closed: Saturday,
Sunday, August, holidays
Nearest Metro:
Faidherbe-Chaligny (8)
Map ref: 3

If you feel hungry and yearn for a traditional French meal in an old-fashioned wood-panelled bistro where the welcome will be warm and genuine, then *A Sousceyrac* is well worth the journey. It is a family business and Monsieur Gabriel Asfaux, who inherited the restaurant from his father, is clearly a proud and happy man, secure in the knowledge that his two sons – one in the kitchen and the other out front – will carry on the business when he is gone. He has the rare quality too, of being able to make you feel that life is worth living, simply by his smile and his handshake.

The menu is painstakingly handwritten each day on a card which, although large, has room for nothing else. The only concession to progress is the fact that copies are then duplicated – in the old days it must have been even more of a mammoth task. Deciphering the violet ink is helped by a Kir – either *ordinaire* or *Royale*. There will be a few bottles of house wine listed, brought up for the day in readiness, and always good value. A separate list is available, with Bordeaux and Burgundies on one side and lesser wines – Cahors especially – on the other, along with some old Armagnacs and other liqueurs. It is an interesting list, not confined to recent vintages as is so often the case in France, and some of the wines are available to take away.

The food is not for the faint-hearted; *terrine* of *foie gras*, hot *saucisson* with wild mushrooms, *cassoulet*, and on Friday nights from early October until just before Christmas, *lièvre à la royale* – a wild hare stew which is a speciality of the restaurant and a gastronomic 'must' if you have never tasted it before.

Monsieur Asfaux takes the orders, giving great deliberation to any question; particularly as to whether or not one dish should follow another, and keeps a fatherly eye on your well-being from the moment you arrive until it is time to leave, when he enquires solicitously if you have far to go, expressing the hope that one day you will return; a hope that must be fulfilled many times over in the course of a year.

12ᵉ ARRONDISSEMENT

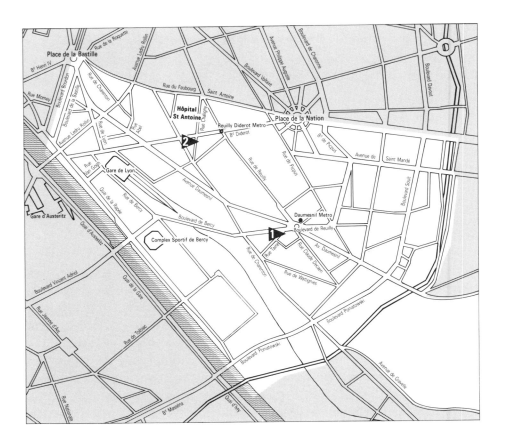

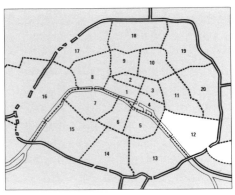

1. Au Trou Gascon
2. Le Morvan

For a nation who on the surface often give every appearance of being undisciplined, the French are very priority minded. The people waiting at this bus stop resolutely refuse to form a queue, but woe betide the one who attempts to board the next *autobus* before his or her rightful turn.

And once the bus is on its way there will be notices setting out other priorities. Seating entitlement for old-age pensioners, pregnant women and war-wounded is only one. There is also a sign stating that in the event of an argument over whether or not a window should be open, the driver will be the sole arbiter; as if he hadn't got enough on

his plate already, supervising the flashing of innumerable passes and the validation of tickets, whilst negotiating the traffic which constantly streams in all directions round the fountain in the middle of the Place Felix Eboué – a square so vast it is practically a bus ride in itself to get from one side to the other.

West of the Place Felix Eboué, along the Avenue Daumesnil and to the right along the Passage Comman, is the Place d'Aligre where since 1843 there has been a street market. More manageable and cheaper than the better-known *Marché aux Puces* (fleamarket) at the Porte de Clignancourt, it is also open every day of the week except Monday (09.30–13.00). Bargain hunters will find old postcards, buttons, and a whole range of oddities amongst the objets d'art.

But if you are approaching it along the Avenue Daumesnil, beware of straying into the area on the left near the Gare de Lyon. At the time of writing it is the centre of the Paris drug trade, and although there is a large police presence from time to time, they aren't always around and a lot of the inhabitants need money quickly and have no qualms about how they get it or whom they hurt in the process.

To the east of Place Felix Eboué, at No. 293 Avenue Daumesnil, by the main entrance to the Bois de Vincennes, is the Musée des Arts Africains et Océaniens (closed Tuesdays), easily identified by a huge basrelief on the main façade recording the contribution made by former French colonies and territories to the mother country and to civilization as a whole.

Street market – Place d'Aligre.

Inside there is a fine collection of ethnic art, including bark paintings, sculptures, pottery, bronzes, rugs and embroidery; whilst in the basement there is an excellent tropical aquarium complete with crocodiles.

Unlike the crocodiles, the attendants are friendly and helpful.

A stone's-throw away, in the Avenue Ste Marie, is the Musée des Transports Urbains (open Saturdays and Sundays, 15 April – 31 October, 14.30–18.00). Run as a labour of love by a group of

enthusiastic amateurs in a former RATP bus depot, it is an exercise in nostalgia, for the collection contains not only all the things that one might expect in the way of old Paris omnibuses with their open platforms at the back, horse-drawn carriages and Metro cars, but unlikely vehicles from other countries as well.

All of which is a suitable prelude for a visit to the Bois de Vincennes. Originally, in the twelfth century, a hunting forest owned by Philippe Auguste, it was given to Paris in 1860 by Napoleon III as part of his policy to promote greenery in the city. Less chic than its rival on the other side of Paris, it nevertheless has as much to offer scenically within its 2,273 acres, and one could happily spend several days exploring the woods, lakes, gardens and other attractions.

To the left, as you enter from the Avenue Daumesnil, is the main Paris zoo, the largest in France and in its time a model for other zoos with its spacious enclosures for the inhabitants. In the centre there is a 235 foot high artificial rock which can be ascended by means of a lift. From the top you can watch the Barbary sheep and mountain goats watching the antics of the penguins in the pool at the foot, or enjoy the fine view of the rest of the Bois de Vincennes.

Past the zoo, again along the Avenue Daumesnil, is the Château and Fort de Vincennes. It began life as a manor house for the use of Philippe Auguste, and was later enlarged by St Louis, who added a Holy Chapel. The castle itself, with its battlements and its magnificent keep surrounded by a moat and drawbridge, was completed in the fourteenth century by Charles V, who also began work on enlarging the Holy Chapel.

Over the years the castle has served as a royal residence, a mediaeval prison for opponents of the monarchy, an arsenal, a small-arms factory, and a fashionable porcelain factory which became so successful that it was eventually transferred to Sèvres.

In 1422 King Henry V of England died of dysentery in the Royal Bed-chamber. The Marquis de Sade served his sentence in the prison. During the last war it was used as a supply depot by the Germans, and in 1944, shortly before they fled, they executed twenty-six members of the French Resistance before blowing up part of the castle ramparts and setting fire to the Queen's Pavilion.

South of the Fort is the Parc Floral de Paris. Originally created for the 1969 Flower Show, it has now become a permanent feature with its magnificent seasonal displays of azaleas, roses and herbaceous plants. Apart from water and medicinal gardens, there is also a small lake, a children's play area, riding stables and restaurant.

Adjoining the area is another, much larger lake, the Lac des Minimes (named after a monastery which once occupied the site). There are three islands, one of which – Porte Jaune – has a café and boats for hire, and can be reached by footbridge.

Continuing on round the Bois in a clockwise direction, past the Indo-Chinese Memorial Temple and Tropical Gardens, one comes to the Ecole du Breuil – a school of horticulture and landscape design – where there are more gardens and an arboretum (closed weekends). Nearby is the Vincennes race-course where trotting races are frequently held.

Back near the main entrance and the zoo is the largest lake in the Bois de Vincennes – Lac Daumesnil. On the two islands, which are connected and can be reached by means of a bridge, there is yet another café, more boats, and bicycles can be hired. In the spring there is a Gingerbread Fair nearby, which lasts for several weeks.

South of the lake is the Municipal Velodrome Cycle Track and a

Buddhist Centre containing a vast fibreglass statue of Buddha covered in gold leaf. For those interested in statistics, the roof tiles – 180,000 of them – were carved by axe out of a single chestnut tree.

Lovers of French bread, or for that matter any bakers who happen to be in the Bois de Vincennes on a Tuesday or Thursday afternoon, might be interested in the Musée Française du Pain at No. 25 *bis* Rue Victor Hugo (south of the cycle track, near the Charenton Ecoles Metro station). It casts its net wide and doesn't confine itself to *baguettes* and *ficelles* through the ages.

Everything one could possibly think of to do with bread is represented: cartoons, knives, signs, shop fronts, model ovens, manuscripts, religious items – altogether a fascinating collection – and it's free!

Entrance to the Bread Museum.

South from the Place Felix Eboué is the deserted area of Bercy, once the centre of the Paris wine trade. Bisected by the Rue de Dijon, the tiny, leafy cobbled streets with evocative and romantic-sounding names like Cour de Barsac, Cour St Emilion, Rue de St Estèphe, Rue de Pommard and Château Lafite, stand sad and empty, awaiting the arrival of the bulldozer. In place of the little one- and two-storey offices and warehouses which once echoed to the sound of smacking lips and clinking glasses, there will be multi-storey concrete office blocks. Such is the price of progress.

A foretaste of things to come is the Complexe Sportif de Bercy, which stands to the west of the old Wine Centre. Built on a grand scale, the acres of wide concrete steps surrounding it provide a setting

A deserted street in the Bercy area – once the centre of the Paris wine trade.

Complexe Sportif de Bercy.

much used by photographers; wedding groups suddenly materialize *en masse* and then just as suddenly disappear again; international choirs congregate; fashion designers turn up with their latest creations.

The near vertical outside is covered by real grass off which pigeons with a head for heights uneasily feed. One waits in vain to see how it is cut. Does a man in blue overalls lower a lawnmower on a rope at the dead of night, or is there some vast, remotely controlled computerized device made specially for the job by the architect's uncle? Perhaps they simply rely on the pigeons? One mourns again the passing of Jacques Tati. He would have had the patience to find out and then made a film about it.

One place unlikely to change in the foreseeable future is the restaurant *Le Train Bleu*, situated one floor up from the main concourse of the Gare de Lyon. In 1972 it was declared a National Monument and received a preservation order. You enter its portals either by lift at the front of the station or, better still, rather more grandly up the staircase inside. Neither way prepares you for what lies ahead. To eat there is an architectural experience almost as enriching as the predominantly Lyonnaise food itself.

Light from a profusion of chandeliers illuminates the snow-white table-cloths and the sparkling silver and glassware. Hardly a square inch of the walls and ceiling is left undecorated. Sculptured panelling covered with murals depicting the journey south through France adorns the walls, rich red velvet curtains frame the arched windows, and from above scantily clad Rubenesque female forms hang to watch over it all.

It is an experience which should not be missed, and on a summer evening as you sit in the window and gaze down at the platforms while passengers board the night train to Nice and beyond, it is all too easy to indulge in flights of fancy about who they are and where they are going and what stories they could tell if only you had the courage to ask. Is the rather sad, beautifully dressed lady with the expensive luggage and no one there to wave her goodbye travelling south to join her lover? Or is she being packed away for the summer months, in the French manner, by a husband who has already joined his mistress? Or both? Or vice versa?

Such notions will scarcely disturb the tranquillity of the elderly waiters, who have doubtless seen it all too often before to give it a second thought. They are more concerned that the leg of lamb *forézienne* with *pommes dauphinois* are to your liking. The chances are that they will be.

40 Rue Taine
Tel: 43.44.34.26
Cards: VISA
Closed: Saturday,
Sunday
Nearest Metro:
Daumesnil (6, 8)
Map ref: 1

The shadow of Monsieur Alain Dutournier's moustache no longer falls on the clients of *Au Trou Gascon*. It has been transported along with its owner to the more salubrious – and expensive! – 1st arrondissement (the *Carré des Feuillants* at 14, Rue de Castiglione). Consequently, the toques and stars in *Gault-Millau* and *Michelin* have been temporarily withdrawn. However, little else seems to have changed, and under Madame Dutournier's direction accolades will doubtless be restored in the fullness of time. The setting is a turn-of-the-century bistro, once a favourite haunt of taxi-drivers, and the atmosphere, like the food, is a mixture of Paris chic and old Gascon.

Monsieur Dutournier is an inventor whose workshop happens to be the kitchen, and if his deputy follows in his footsteps, then each day will bring its surprises; a marriage of ravioli with *foie gras* perhaps, or lobster with ginger. Inspiration comes with what is available in the market on a particular day, so other than mentioning delights from Gascony, like Landes chicken with asparagus, Chalosse ham, or the ubiquitous *cassoulet*, it is impossible to single out dishes, for they won't necessarily be on the menu.

The vast annotated wine list makes exciting reading, and it is worth getting there early just for that, and to round off the meal there is a suitably long list of vintage Armagnacs.

NB Monsieur Dutournier has also joined forces with three other distinguished Paris chefs; Bernard Fournier of *Le Petit Colombier*, Jean-Pierre Morot-Gaudry and Henri Faugeron, and together they own a wine bar, *Le Pain et le Vin*, at 1 Rue d'Armaille in the 17th arrondissement. (Closed Saturdays and Sundays. Nearest Metro: Argentine (1).) There they serve wines from most areas of France along with various sandwiches, salads, plates of smoked salmon or cheese, and a changing *plat du jour*.

22 Rue Chaligny
Tel: 43.07.47.66
Cards: None
Closed: Saturday,
Sunday, August
Nearest Metro: Reuilly-
Diderot (1, 8)
Map ref: 2

It would probably be stretching things a bit to say that *Le Morvan* is worth a journey right across Paris, when one would pass so many other good restaurants on the way. However, if you have cause to be in the 12th arrondissement, it is most certainly worth a detour, particularly at lunchtime, when you will suddenly find yourself caught up in the hustle and bustle of a good, honest restaurant which gives excellent value for money, and is crowded with the kind of serious eaters who take their jackets off the better to enjoy their meal.

There is a patterned stone floor, a large polished wood bar, paper cloths on the tables, and brisk, but friendly and caring attention from the owners, Monsieur and Madame Guyard, who are an object lesson on how to serve a packed dining-room without ever keeping anyone waiting or making it appear that they are anything other than happy in being at times grossly over-worked.

And what do the regulars eat? *Escargots* bubbling away in juice you can smell from the other side of the room, duck in cucumber and cream, *lapin dijonnais,* steaks; all cooked to perfection by the chef, Jean-Claude Prieur, and accompanied by delicious *pommes allumettes.* Wine from Burgundy comes in *pichets* or by the bottle, and there are a couple of red Bordeaux listed.

Across the hall of the apartment block there is a very basic toilet of Imperial dimensions.

If you are in the mood for that kind of restaurant, you would have to travel a long way to find a better one, but you will need to book.

13ᵉ Arrondissement

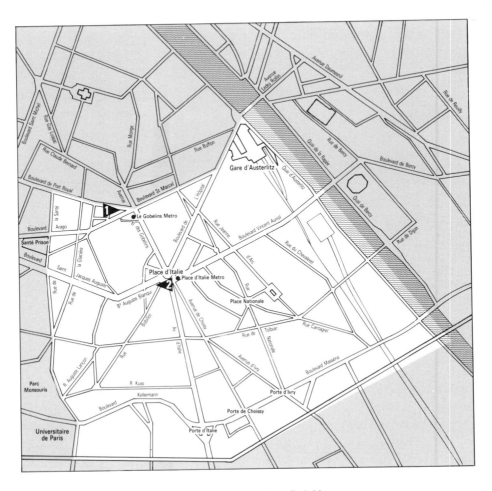

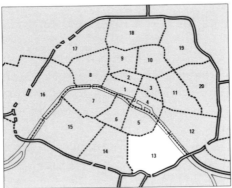

1. Le Petit Marguery
2. Les Vieux Métiers de France

At No. 61, Boulevard Arago, beneath a canopy of old chestnut trees, lies the Cité Fleurie. With its narrow lanes and half-timbered houses set in countrified lawns and gardens, it is one of the oldest surviving artists' colonies in Paris. Gauguin lived here for a while after he returned from Tahiti, and a plate on the entrance gates records the fact that between 1934 and 1940 it was a repository for books by anti-Nazi writers.

'Don't look now,' said the horse, 'but I think someone is trying to take our photograph.'

'Cock-a-doodle-doo!' cried the hen. 'Doesn't he know this is private property? Pretend you haven't seen anything. Perhaps he'll go away.'

Taking pictures of the house next door to the Cité Fleurie – known officially as the Maison d'Arrêt de la Santé – causes even more of a flurry. This old *vespasienne* was the nearest the gendarme on duty would allow me to get to photographing France's once notorious gaol, and even taking this picture was viewed with suspicion. Perhaps he thought I was going to pass it on to one of the inmates as a possible hiding-place in the event of an escape. In fact, he did me a service, for it is much more photogenic than the grim old walls of the prison, and it must be one of the very few old-fashioned urinals left in Paris now. The rest have been consigned to a muncipal dump in St Denis, having been replaced by space-age unisex *sanisettes*; all concrete and steel.

Viewed by the inmates of the prison through their cell bars, it must, with its leafy surroundings, seem like a haven of peace; a symbol of the freedom they once enjoyed.

That the French have a great addiction to tapestry work cannot be denied. Witness the vast array of materials and designs on sale in haberdashery shops up and down the country – *someone* must buy them all.

Undoubtedly some of the greatest practitioners in the world are alive and well and working away at the rate of an area not much larger than a postage stamp per day at the Manufacture des Gobelins at No. 42, Avenue des Gobelins. (Open to the public on Wednesdays, Thursdays and Fridays, when there are guided tours conducted by highly knowledgeable specialist lecturers from the Caisse des Monuments Historiques.)

The factory, indeed the whole area, owes its name to Jean Gobelin, a Flemish dyer specializing in scarlet, who around the year 1440 set up his workshop on the banks of the river Bièvre, using cochineal brought over from India. The business prospered, and when in 1660, during the reign of Louis XIV, the then Minister of Finance, Colbert, was given the task of grouping together all the tapestry *ateliers* in Paris in order to create 'The Royal Factory of Tapestry and Carpet Weavers to the Crown', he bought 'Les Gobelins' – house, gardens, meadows and adjoining woods – and in so doing immortalized the family name.

The King's principal painter, Charles le Brun, whose statue stands just inside the entrance, was appointed manager of the factory and charged with creating designs for the Royal household. The house in which he lived and worked is one of the few original buildings remaining.

Although most of the present factory was built as recently as 1912, the looms and the method of weaving have remained virtually unchanged. The weavers still work at upright looms, stitching on to the reverse side of the canvas, working always in daylight to a picture which is mounted behind them and reflected by means of mirrors. They have nearly fifteen thousand different shades of colour at their disposal, and over the years many famous artists, from Le Brun to Picasso, have supplied the designs. Each tapestry takes between four and five years to complete, and since the factory first opened over five thousand have been woven.

The tour takes you past a statue of Colbert, the original factory chapel – now deconsecrated and housing two tapestries on permanent display – the dye works, which has been there since 1665, the weaving school and the Rue Berbier-du-Mets, under which the Bièvre still flows on its way to the Seine. A little further on, beyond the National Furniture Depository, is a modern block which houses the Manufacture de la Savonnerie and the Manufacture de Beauvais. The former, which occupies the first two floors, specializes in carpets and has been part of the Gobelins since 1826. It began life in 1663 when Colbert moved a carpet factory from the Louvre into a soap factory on a site which is now occupied by the Museum of Modern Art. Here the weavers work from the front of the loom, with their backs to the light.

The Gobelins' Tapestry Factory.

The Manufacture de Beauvais originally made tapestries, chair coverings and other woven items for private sale, working on horizontal looms. It joined the group after its premises in Beauvais were bombarded and destroyed by fire during the last war. Nowadays production from all three factories goes to the state for use in Government buildings.

With its cobbled courtyards, gardens and apartments for the workers, many of whom start work there at an early age and remain for the rest of their lives, the atmosphere at the Manufacture des Gobelins is more like a monastery or a college than a factory.

Paris is a city of contrasts, and the 13th provides some good – or bad – examples of this.

In 1974 President Giscard d'Estaing called a temporary halt to high-rise development; a decision France Soir celebrated with the banner headlines – LES TOURS A PARIS: C'EST FINI.

The President underlined his policy by stating that 'the city must remain familiar to all' – a view which millions the world over would have echoed, not least around the Place d'Italie, known to the planners as 'Ilot 4'. Unfortunately, he arrived on the scene too late to stop the work of his predecessors, and vast areas around the Rue Nationale, once a bustling, thriving, self-contained quarter of Paris, had already been razed to the ground.

And as the area went up in the world in the physical sense, so it rose socially too, and its very nature changed. The old inhabitants, unable to afford the higher rents, moved out to a healthier, but not necessarily happier life in the suburbs, while new ones moved in.

Perhaps the latter now sit in their boxes dreaming of rose-filled gardens, whilst the former dream of life as it used to be before the little shops gave way to giant *supermarchés*. Nothing is perfect, least of all in 'Ilot 4'.

9 Boulevard de Port-Royal
Tel: 43.31.58.59
Cards: AE, DC, EC, VISA
Closed: Sunday, Monday, August, 24 December–2 January
Nearest Metro: Les Gobelins (7)
Map ref: 1

With its barely legible menu written in purple ink, its potted plants, its décor of red, pink and green with murals of balloons in blue superimposed, and its predominantly French clientèle tucking into their food, *Le Petit Marguery* is everyone's idea of what eating out in a typical Paris bistro should be like. It is a happy, friendly place, well worth a detour, as Michelin would say. One hesitates to mention it in a guide for fear of it being spoilt, although hidden away where it is it won't be on many people's itinerary, except for those needing to visit a long-lost relative doing time in the Santé prison just up the road.

As a customer you certainly won't be taken for granted, either by the brothers Alain, Michel and Jacques, or by the waiters in black waistcoats and with their white sleeves rolled up ready for business, who couldn't be nicer or more friendly.

The tone is set by the Kir, which is generous in its measure of cassis. The menu is large and dishes sampled include *cassoulet* of *escargots* with mushrooms, *terrine maison*, and veal with poached eggs, tagliatelle and toast heavily soaked with garlic; the latter sounds lethal, and could be if taken to excess, but tastes delicious.

The wine list spreads its net far and wide, covering most regions of France. If you happen to collect wine labels, Château Marquisat de Binet has a lovely picture of an outhouse which somehow goes with the food as well as the restaurant. The contents are very drinkable too.

Perhaps the only criticism might be of an occasional heavy-handedness with the pepperpot in the kitchen.

13 Boulevard Auguste Blanqui
Tel: 45.88.40.03
Cards: AE, DC, EC, VISA
Closed: Sunday, Monday
Nearest Metro: Place D'Italie (5, 6, 7)
Map ref: 2

A slight odd-ball of a restaurant, at first sight *Les Vieux Métiers de France* makes one pause for thought, wondering if the journey has been worthwhile, for given its surroundings the outside has to be less *vieux* than it looks. But once inside, and settled in the equally fake, but very elegantly constructed, interior, these qualms are soon forgotten; at least the stone is real and the woodwork genuine.

Appetizers of mussels served in a curry sauce sharpen the appetite along with the Kir. There is a reasonably priced 'gourmet' menu, but if the portions are as large as those served *à la carte* then it might be wise to get into training first.

Recommended are the *papillote du foie gras aux choux*, the *terrine, baron de lapereau à la moutarde* and *noisettes d'agneau* with *tartine* (fried bread heavily soaked in garlic is very popular in the 13th!). To end with there is delicious *tarte légère aux pommes*.

Monsieur Moisan is a keen oenophile and keeps a cellar of some 20,000 bottles, which you are welcome to inspect. The wine list itself makes good reading and contains temptations at all prices.

Les Vieux Métiers de France is a comfortable and welcoming restaurant where you can spend the evening without feeling at all pressurized, and to which one would always happily return. The waiters seem unusually tall and elegant.

14ᵉ ARRONDISSEMENT

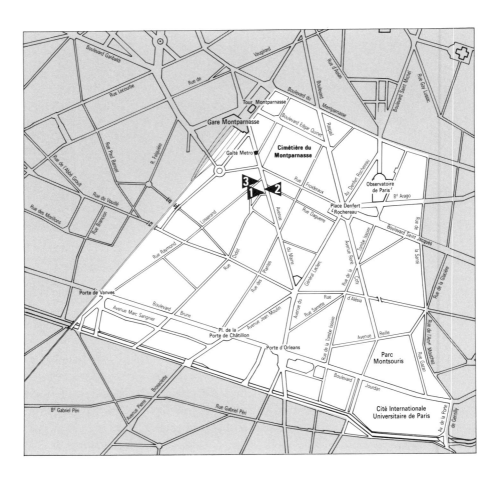

1. Chez Albert
2. Les Armes de Bretagne
3. Au Feu Follet

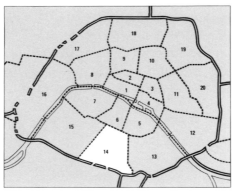

When the Parc de Montsouris was officially opened in the late 1870s, the lake sprung a leak and all the water ran away. The engineer responsible was so mortified he committed suicide. Nowadays he would most likely blame the plumber and there would be a strike. People don't care that much any more.

Montsouris literally means 'the hill of mice' and it gained its name because before Baron Haussman took it in hand it was a site for granaries.

It is one of the prettiest of Paris parks, its forty or so acres much painted by Picasso's friend, the customs officer Rousseau, when he lived nearby. In the centre of the park there is a rather unlikely reproduction of the Bey's Palace in Tunis, erected for the 1876 Exhibition and now used as a meteorological observatory – Paris is full of surprises.

In the 1930s for most people the name 'Montparnasse' meant the Boulevard du Montparnasse and that in turn meant *La Coupole*. Opened on 20 December 1927, the restaurant rapidly became a centre for intellectual life in the area. Anyone who was anyone went there at one time or another, to see or be seen. Josephine Baker even used to take her ocelot with her (on a lead). Hemingway, Gertrude Stein and Henry Miller frequented it regularly, along with others of the pre-war American literary set.

Recently there have been plans to turn it into a cinema, like the old Rotonde, so if you want to relive the past beneath the famous frescoes it might be as well to go soon.

At the beginning of the last war philosophy took over from art. Led by Jean-Paul Sartre, the exodus north to the warmer and friendlier Boulevard Saint Germain began. It was a move which was aided and abetted by the occupying German army who took over *La Coupole* and its rivals, *Le Sélect*, *Le Dôme* and *La Rotonde*, adding insult to injury by bringing their own coffee.

Then, after the war, having witnessed the signing of the German Military Governor's surrender, the old Gare Monparnasse in the

*La Coupole in the
Boulevard de
Montparnasse.*

adjacent 15th was pulled down and the Tour Montparnasse began to rise up in its place. Not only was the sun setting on Boulevard du Montparnasse as the hub of Bohemian Paris, it was replaced by the shadow of the new 656 foot high tower.

However, the feeling of doom which is left around the Avenue du Maine hasn't yet spread to the heart of the neighbourhood, which is where the Boulevard Raspail crosses the Boulevard du Montparnasse, and where Rodin's statue of Balzac stands. Traditionally, the area is much populated by Bretons, for the railway line connects with north-western France. Fish restaurants proliferate, as do cafés specializing in cider and *crêpes*. Even the prostitutes speak with a Breton accent, for girls who travel to the big city in search of easy money seldom move far from the station at which they arrived.

Montparnasse is to the left bank what Montmartre was to the

right. Montmartre suffered too many tourists and changed; Mont-parnasse has suffered from the war and soulless redevelopment. It got its name in the seventeenth-century after Mount Parnassus – the mountain sacred to Apollo and the Muses – because of the mound on which it stood. But the mound has been flattened and now the muses have mostly left. The Rue de la Gaîté, once the centre of theatreland, no longer lives up to its name – but Baudelaire, Maupassant, César Franck and Saint-Saens lie undisturbed in the Cimetière Mont-parnasse, although watched over now by the occupants of tower blocks.

Further south along the Boulevard Raspail is the Place Denfert-Rochereau, and the entrance to the catacombs (every Saturday afternoon between 1 July and 15 October, and every third Saturday of the month for the rest of the year). The whole visit takes about three quarters of an hour, and it is hard to say whether it is worth doing or not, but in the tourist season there is usually a queue of people who obviously expect it to be. In essence the catacombs are former stone quarries which are now filled with ossified remains taken from Paris cemeteries during the eighteenth and nineteenth centuries; tunnel after tunnel lined with neatly stacked piles of bones and what one assumes to be a matching number of skulls – enough to make up between five and six million complete skeletons. It is a slightly eerie feeling, walking along underground accompanied by occasional dis-embodied voices and strange rumbles from overhead. The stone buildings at the entrance house the Inspector General of Quarries and were once a toll gate – a reminder that the original wall around Paris

was built not so much to keep people out as to make them pay for the privilege of coming in.

In the south-east corner of the arrondissement, beyond the Parc de Montsouris, is the Cité Universitaire, a series of well laid out hostels for students of all nationalities, two of which – the Swiss Foundation and the Franco-Brazilian – were designed by Le Corbusier.

But now we are back in the Parc de Montsouris, where nothing much has changed since Lenin lived in the area and used to meet fellow exiled revolutionaries on their mornings off. True, there is talk of restoring the Bey's Palace and turning it into a Tunisian Cultural Centre, but pigeons still watch hopefully as an old man makes his way slowly home carrying his shopping bag.

As with most Paris parks, there is a good restaurant at hand, for instance Le Jardin de la Paresse – the Garden of Leisure (open May till October). With luck a band might be playing in the nearby bandstand, and if you happen to have children with you they can play in the sandpit between courses of the special 'children's lunch', while you sit under the trees and watch the ducks and swans glide past. All very bucolic and peaceful.

Parc de Montsouris.

122 Avenue du Maine
Tel: 43.20.21.69
Cards: AE, CB, DC, EC
Closed: Monday,
Saturday lunch, 12–26
August
Nearest Metro: Gaîté
(13)
Map ref: 1

The elderly and avuncular Monsieur Marcel Beaumont watches over every detail in this old restaurant, anxious to give pleasure and thoroughly delighted when he does – which is often. With his shiny face and whispy white hair he reminds one irresistibly of Stéphane Grappelli; so much so one wouldn't be at all surprised if he suddenly produced a violin from behind his back and serenaded you over the duck pâté – a speciality which was being singled out for star rating by *Michelin* nearly forty years ago.

Sitting in the 'terrace' area, with its ceiling draped in hanging folds of silken material, gives one an inkling of what it must be like to be a middle-eastern potentate, which is what you need to be if you succumb to some of the higher-priced top growth clarets on the wine list rather than the excellent examples from the Jura. It also leads one to wonder how such restaurants manage to annexe whole areas of pavement, and what, in the eyes of the authorities, constitutes a temporary rather than a permanent structure.

Browsing through old copies of the *Guide Michelin*, dishes like *coquille St Jacques en brochette, homard poché aux herbes, carré d'agneau aux aromates* and *estouffade Bourguignonne* have an air of permanence about them too. One can almost picture the Inspectors, their taste buds throbbing as they made their way up the Rue du Maine in order to pay their annual respects. Sadly, something must have gone wrong on their last visit, for after many years in the firmament, the star has disappeared.

However, that shouldn't stop anyone going. It happened once before in the early fifties and they fought back. No doubt the same thing will happen again. When restaurants like *Chez Albert* disappear a way of life will disappear too, and the French are much too fond of life to let that kind of thing happen.

108 Avenue du Maine
Tel: 43.20.29.50
Cards: AE, DC, EC,
VISA
Closed: Sunday evening,
Mondays except holidays,
first week in January,
26 April–5 May,
4–24 August
Nearest Metro: Gaîté
(13)
Map ref: 2

From the moment the doorman, resplendent in his semi-naval uniform, ushers you through the portals and you are virtually 'piped' aboard, the sea is never far away. The setting of the dining-room is in the style of Napoleon III, and large sea-snails are served with the Kir, so it is not for those who are squeamish when confronted by unfamiliar denizens of the ocean bed. Nor will things improve if you order lobster, for it will be brought to your table fresh from the tank for approval before being roasted in whichever of several different ways you happen to prefer. Scallops come with fresh pasta, and sole with chives.

Les Armes de Bretagne also specializes in duck, cooked in six different ways, including a version with pink peppercorns.

The *carte* is fixed and laminated, but extras are occasionally attached. It is also, as far as the lobster is concerned, unpriced – as is so often the case with a creature which takes so long to mature and is so sought after. The wine list is good but not cheap.

In England, *Les Armes de Bretagne* would be an expense account restaurant catering mainly for businessmen. In France it still caters for businessmen, but it is also a restaurant where ordinary people go, and because they are paying cash they demand and get high quality of the old order.

5 Rue Raymond-
Losserand
Tel: 43.22.65.72
Cards: None
Closed: Lunchtime,
Sunday, 12–20 August
Nearest Metro: Gaîté
Map ref: 3

Au Feu Follet first came to my attention through a series of misprints in *Atlas*, the otherwise impeccably produced Air France in-flight magazine: 'An old-fashioned cooking with a father day taste to be find out, plain but excellent.' It was hard to resist.

It is a tiny restaurant at the back of the new Gare Montparnasse, made to feel even smaller by an abundance of plants and flowers, along with wall decorations and some strange hanging lamps adorned with what look like old pink napkins, but I knew I was going to like it the moment I phoned to book a table. For some reason Bond isn't an easy name to say over the telephone; it gets translated into anything from Sand to Bent and usually necessitates peering at the reservations book on arrival at a restaurant in order to lay claim to a table. I sometimes swallow hard and mention my illustrious name-sake. The possibility of my being James Bond sent the voice at the other end into paroxysms of happy laughter. It boded well for the food and I wasn't disappointed.

Au Feu Follet is a friendly place, almost casual; one gets the feeling that many of the clients are personal friends of Odette Bilhourd, which gives it something of the atmosphere of a pre-war bistro. The menu is short, with perhaps a greater emphasis on first rather than main courses. The bacon quiche looks stodgy, but turns out to be very edible indeed, and can be followed by dishes like ham with lentil and vegetable purée or veal. In short, it is 'home cooking', but of dishes one might not normally cook at home. Perhaps Air France had it right all the time.

The wine list is small and reasonably priced; homely wines to accompany homely dishes. A red Saumur went down very well on the last occasion.

Not necessarily worthy of a journey across Paris, but re-commended if you happen to be in the area and feel like a quiet, unexotic meal in kindly surroundings.

15ᵉ ARRONDISSEMENT

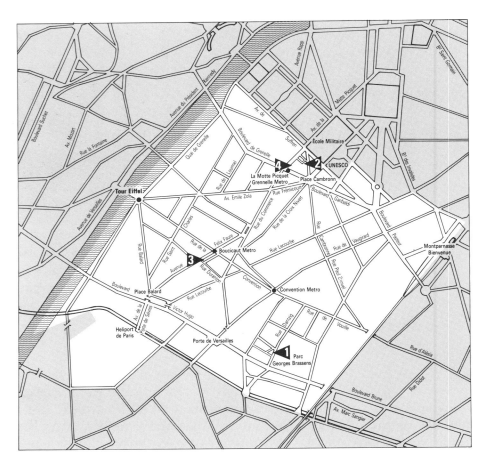

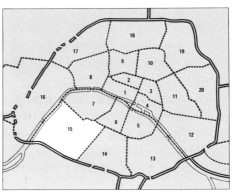

1. L'Aquitaine
2. Morot-Gaudry
3. Pierre Vedel
4. La Gauloise

General de Gaulle's gift to France was to pull it up by its bootstrings and give it a new sense of pride. Under his guidance it became a cleaner place. Plumbing underwent a revolution. The railway system was rebuilt and fast, modern trains ran on time. The antiquated telephone system was transformed. He encouraged the French people to take a giant leap into the twentieth century, and they responded whole-heartedly. Despite their individualistic approach to life, they like to be led and to know where they stand.

But there is a price to pay for everything, and the Tour Montparnasse, rising like a giant tombstone above the old cemetery, was part of that price. In another setting it would be an object of admiration, but in the 15th arrondissement it is an anachronism, a monument to man's inability always to come to terms with progress.

The tallest office block in Europe, its 39,000 square metres of glass and 120,000 tons of masonry house over 7,000 workers, as well as a vast complex of department stores, restaurants, swimming pools and squash courts.

The best thing that can be said about the Tour Montparnasse is that on a clear day there is a lovely view from the top, and at night it can be quite magical. In less than forty seconds, high speed lifts whisk you non-stop to the 56th floor, where there is an observatory with an illuminated frieze running round the top of the wall and a spoken commentary in six languages to help you pick out the various landmarks. There is also a bar and a restaurant, although the latter, like many similar establishments the world over, trades on its unique situation for its custom.

Two floors higher (by foot) you can see the same view but from the open roof top. It is all much easier and more civilized than the Eiffel Tower, and at two hundred metres almost as high.

Behind the Tour Montparnasse is the Gare Montparnasse, moved a long way back from its original site, a fact worth remembering if you have a train to catch and get off the Metro at Montparnasse Bienvenu with only minutes to spare. Paris's most modern main-line terminus, it is a permanent reminder that railway architecture is no longer what it was in the grand old days of steam. Not, in Michelin parlance, worth a detour.

Paris at night from the top of the Tour Montparnasse.

Certainly worth a detour, although equally modern, is the Musée de la Poste across the Boulevard Vaugirard at No. 34. Thoughtfully laid out, you start at the fifth floor with a short film and then gradually make your way downstairs through a series of rooms where lights come on automatically as you enter and which contain beautifully displayed exhibits covering almost every aspect relating to the posting and delivery of letters through the ages, many of which you probably wouldn't even have thought of. There is something for everyone, not just philatelists; model planes and boats, coaches, uniforms, boots from different periods, nagivational instruments, printing machines, engravings, automatic sorting machines, calendars, stamps galore, and occasional exhibitions of the works of contemporary artists involved in their design.

Another museum worth a visit while you are in the area is the Musée Bourdelle (closed Mondays, free on Sundays). Situated almost exactly behind the Postal Museum, at No. 16 Rue Antoine Bourdelle, it contains a collection of some 2,500 examples of his work, ranging from paintings and sketches to monumental sculptures standing in the garden and courtyard. Emile Bourdelle, known as Antoine, and at one time a protégé of Rodin, lived and worked at No. 16 for forty-five years until his death in 1929. The studio was given to the City of Paris by his wife and daughter in 1948, and has been left exactly as it was when he died, complete with furniture made by him and his father, who was a cabinet maker. A good time to visit the museum is in the spring or early summer, when the somewhat overgrown garden is at its best.

At the southern end of the arrondissement, along the Rue Danzig, is an entrance to the Parc Georges Brassens, built on the site of the old Vaugirard slaughterhouse, one of whose victims served as a model for Soutine's masterpiece 'The Slayed Steer'. Shortly before you reach it, on the right hand side of the Rue Danzig, is the Passage Danzig, and you can see where Soutine lived and worked in La Ruche, a strange rotunda-shaped building with an oriental pagoda style roof. Set in a garden overflowing with shrubs and trees, behind a pair of enormous Art Nouveau wrought-iron gates, it is still a thriving artists' colony, and if you care to wander round no-one will stop you.

La Ruche, an artists' colony in the Passage Danzig.

It owes its existence to the sculptor Boucher who, after the 1900 World Fair, bought up some of the old buildings including the wine pavilion and had them re-erected on the present site by the same team who constructed the Eiffel Tower. It was opened in 1902 and at its peak contained about two hundred studios – hence the name 'Ruche', meaning 'beehive'.

Chagall lived here along with Soutine and other famous artists like Leger, Zadkini and Modigliani.

Its latter-day history is not dissimilar to other such colonies in Paris. In 1965 it was bought up by a property developer who had thoughts of replacing it with a tower block and underground garages. André Malraux, then Minister of Culture, stepped in and blocked the building permit, allowing time for funds to be raised in order to buy it back. At the same time it was classified as an historical monument. Nowadays some fifty artists live there in relative comfort.

Flying over the centre of Paris purely for pleasure is strictly *interdit*, but if you feel like a ten or twenty minute bird's-eye view of what it looks like from two thousand feet just inside the Périphérique (the view here is of Porte St Cloud shortly after take-off), then a visit to the Paris heliport at 4 Avenue de la Porte-de-Sèvres can be thoroughly recommended. It isn't cheap, but pro rata it compares favourably with going up the Eiffel Tower and it is a memorable experience. If you get really hooked on the sensation, as well you might, there are longer excursions to Versailles and the Loire Valley, although for the latter you will need to dig fairly deeply into your pocket.

There is a minimum payload of four passengers and you should telephone beforehand to Héli-location on 45.58.44.22 or 45.57.66.33 to make sure a plane is available. The nearest Metro is: Balard (8).

54 Rue de Danzig
Tel: 48.28.67.38
Cards: AE, DC, EC,
VISA
Closed: Sunday,
Monday
Nearest Metro:
Convention (12)
Map ref: 1

As might be expected from the name, *L'Aquitaine* specializes in food from the south-west corner of France. It is a predominantly female establishment, and Christine Massia, who also turns her talents to teaching other girls to cook, runs what in the navy would be known as a 'tight ship'. The welcome is warm, but in the early part of the evening there can be a certain amount of 'poofing' and pursing of lips. A large blackboard listing the day's specialities is plonked down very firmly on a stand in front of your table, supplementing a menu in which the emphasis is on fish and duck. Ordering from the black-board is rewarded by a ravishing smile – like giving an apple to the teacher – but on the last visit I felt I had lost Brownie points a moment later when I ordered a white Châteauneuf-du-Pape (mainly because I had never drunk one before).

However, as the evening progresses and things settle down all is sweetness and light, and if you arrive early enough to get a table on the first-floor terrace at the rear of the restaurant, which faces the 'Beehive' on the opposite side of the Passage Danzig, there are few more pleasant places to eat on a summer evening in Paris. Large candles and floor lights provide the illumination and one has the feeling of being perhaps part of a scene about to be captured by some latter-day Chagall in one of the studios opposite, perhaps Henri Pelletier, who was responsible for the frescoes on the walls of the main dining-room.

Prices are reasonable, and the cooking is unexpectedly light for a restaurant which has its roots in an area normally associated with fairly robust fare; *salade aux queues de crevette, panaché de poissons au beurre blanc, confit froid de canard, beignets de fromage de chèvre* and *tourtière* – strudel filled with sautéed apples and prunes and served with prune ice-cream, a speciality of the region – are all dishes which have been approved by many guides with the exception of *Gault-Millau.* Coffee is served, rather unexpectedly, by a black man in very impressive robes, who looks and behaves like a visiting dignitary.

8 Rue de la Cavalerie
Tel: 45.67.06.85
Cards: CB, VISA
Closed: Saturday,
Sunday
Nearest Metro: La
Motte Picquet (6, 8, 10)
Map ref: 2

The *Morot-Gaudry* is not the easiest of restaurants to find – mainly because it is situated on the eighth floor of a somewhat anonymous building tucked away at the end of a street which is itself hard to find. But once you have located the entrance and made the journey up by lift, all is forgiven. Through the windows during the winter months, or from the flowered terrace in summer, you can look out across the rooftops towards the Eiffel Tower, which seems only a stone's throw away, while enjoying some of the most inventive cuisine around.

The duck liver, *mousseline* of oysters with vermouth, calf's head with horseradish one day or with raspberries the next, monkfish with crocus pistils, red mullet with *chanterelles*, crab *boudin*, lamb's tongue with sauternes, rice cake with ginger and other desserts, have all been singled out for praise at one time or another, and give an idea of the kind of cuisine to expect; not so much *nouvelle* as idiosyncratically inventive.

There is also an extremely good wine list, and perhaps the best way to enjoy both the food and the wine on a first visit is to partake of the fixed-price *menu-suggestion*, which consists of six different courses with six different wines to accompany them. The row of glasses of different shapes and sizes set out in front of you before the start of the meal is exciting in itself and sets the taste buds throbbing in anticipation of the pleasures to come.

Morot-Gaudry is much patronized by officials from UNESCO, whose offices are not far away, so you will certainly need to book, but it is worth the trouble and the bill won't be horrendous.

19 Rue Duranton
Tel: 45.58.43.17
Cards: None
Closed: Saturday,
Sunday, 7 July–
4 August, one week at
Christmas
Nearest Metro:
Boucicaut (8)
Map ref: 3

With its mirrors and potted palms, its large revolving fans hanging from the ceiling and its painted anaglypta wallpaper, Pierre Vedel's restaurant has something of a *Cage aux Folles* atmosphere about it. It also looks as if it could have been there for ever, but in fact it recently moved from an out-of-the-way address in the same arrondissement, faithful followers and all, and no chef could wish for a greater compliment.

Monsieur Vedel hails from Sète, on the west coast of France, and the cuisine reflects his love for the area. Fish is what he is best at; delicious *bourride* fillet of *rascasse* with saffron, for example, but his particular ability is to add his own touches to classical recipes, and any attempts at *nouvelle cuisine* have more to do with the cooking than with the serving. Vegetables tend to be cooked in with the main ingredient rather than served separately in a pretty pattern on the side plate, and are all the better for it.

A good first course is poached egg with sliced artichoke hearts and a *coulis* of tomato, and meat is certainly not ignored on the menu; *aiguillettes* of duck come with a *tian* of aubergine, veal sweetbreads with a beetroot mousse.

For a patron who was brought up in a fishing port, the wine list seems a bit low on whites; only three are listed – a Muscadet, a Sancerre and a Chablis. On the other hand, when they are good what could be better?

La Gauloise. 59 Avenue de la Motte-Picquet. **Tel:** 47.34.11.64. **Cards:** VISA. **Closed:** Saturday and Sunday. **Nearest Metro:** La Motte Picquet (6, 8, 10). **Map ref:** 5.

Traditional and reliable, the long dining-room of *La Gauloise* has a quiet but solid provincial air which is part of its charm and provides a suitable atmosphere for equally traditional dishes; *navarin* of lamb, *fricassée* of duck, veal sweetbreads and the like. Recommended for a good meal at a reasonable price.

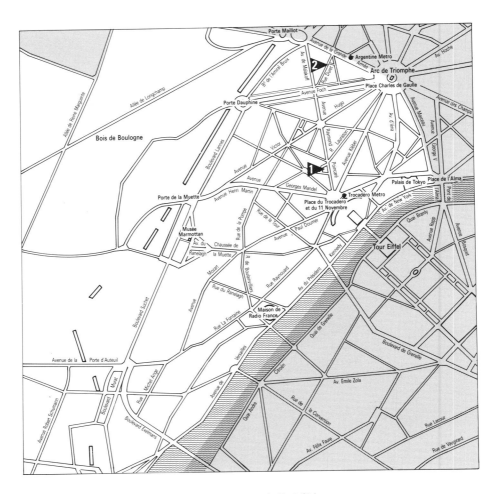

1. Paul Chêne
2. Guy Savoy

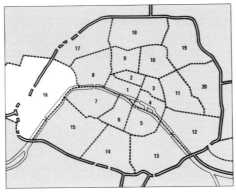

Hide and seek is the same the whole world over. The only difference in this case is that it is being played around La Fontaine Lamartine in the square of the same name.

Here in 1866 a 1,926 foot artesian well was sunk in order to supply water to the lakes in the Bois de Boulogne. Later it became a source of mineral water for the Parisian public. Despite being classified as *non potable* by the Laboratoire du Contrôle des Eaux de

Public fountain in the Square Lamartine.

Roller skating at the Trocadero.

la Ville de Paris, it is still going strong and every day well-to-do hydrophiles armed with plastic bottles and thermos flasks can be seen rubbing shoulders with passing lorry and taxi drivers as they queue to replenish their stocks. Anything which is free and good for the liver can't be totally bad.

Not so far away, on the vast terrace above the Parc du Trocadéro, older brothers demonstrate their prowess on roller skates, performing daring and sometimes terrifying leaps up and down the steps. The terrace also boasts one of the finest views of western Paris. Below it, sloping gardens on either side of a group of fountains lead down to the Seine, and beyond that, on the far side of the river, lies the Parc du Champ. On a warm evening, when the fountains are floodlit, it is a splendid sight. But don't expect to be the only one there, and watch out for strange people lurking in the bushes!

The Place du Trocadéro is also the site of the monumental Palais de Chaillot, which houses many fine museums: the Musée de l'Homme (closed Tuesdays), the Musée des Monuments Français, full of fascinating plaster replicas of early sculptures and reproductions of famous murals – the saving on fares and feet in searching out the originals is considerable (closed Tuesdays), the Musée de la Marine – where there is a marvellous collection of scale models, cannons and navigational instruments (closed Tuesdays), and – best of all if you happen to be an avid cinema-goer – La Musée du Cinéma Henri-Langlois.

Henri Langlois virtually became a squatter in the basement of the Palais in order to establish a home for some five thousand objects out of his private collection of costumes, film sets, special-effects devices, cameras and projectors. The museum is in the Paris wing of the Palais and is reached via a garden path off the Rue de Mun. There are guided tours at set hours every day except Monday.

There are also two theatres with seven daily showings of a constantly changing programme of films, often including rare early silent movies, between 15.00 and 23.00.

The museum isn't easy to find, but that will be remedied in the not too distant future when it moves further along the Avenue du President-Wilson to the Palais de Tokyo, where the west wing is being converted into a National Film Centre, uniting it with many other aspects of the cinema.

The Palais de Tokyo is no longer the home of the National Museum of Modern Art, which has been transferred to the Pompidou Centre, but relies mostly on private donations. There are also a number of post-impressionist works and 'over-flow' paintings from the Louvre. (Closed Tuesdays)

Nearby, at No. 6 Place d'Iéna, is the Musée Guimet, which specializes in Asian arts and houses several collections of early Chinese ceramics and porcelain (closed Tuesdays), while at No. 10 Avenue Pierre-ler-de-Serbie, the Palais Galliéra houses the Musée de la Mode et du Costume with its collection of over 4,000 costumes and 25,000 articles from the wardrobes of men and women of fashion from 1735 onwards. (Closed Mondays)

If you head in a westerly direction from the Palais de Chaillot, along the Rue Franklin, and then past some modern apartment blocks in the Rue Raynouard, you come eventually to No. 47, where there is a gate set in the wall and some steps which lead down to a small house nestling in a leafy garden.

It was in this house in the 1840s that Honoré de Balzac used to

Balzac's house at number 47 Rue Raynouard and the back way out into Rue Berton.

sit up all night in his dressing-gown, ruining his health by drinking gallons of black coffee, while he worked feverishly on his novels in order to keep his many creditors at bay. He called the house 'ma cabane' and rented it under the name of his housekeeper, Louise Breugnot. It was here that he worked on his massive series of novels, *La Comédie Humaine*, and in the garden there is a bas-relief commemorating the fact.

For many years the house was a private museum, but in 1960 it became a Museum of the City of Paris. At first sight the inside seems relatively bare. This is because, after he married Madame Hanska, Balzac took the furniture with him and when they were both dead most of it was disposed of. But like many authors, perhaps he thrived on the pressures.

However, the house has lots of mementoes; the armchair and the table on which he wrote, the famous coffee-pot on its spirit lamp, and many photographs of the women in his life, together with caricatures and a vast collection of unpaid bills, summonses and distraints. One wonders whether, if he had led a more orderly life, the world of literature would have been a poorer place.

Balzac lived in what was then a comparatively remote part of Paris in order to avoid being confronted by his creditors.

At the back of No. 47 Rue Raynouard there is a 'hidden door', an escape route, which opens onto the Rue Berton at a lower level.

The Rue Berton is a quaint little alley-way, more of a country lane; once the haunt of lovers, but now watched over by gendarmes, sub machine-guns at the ready. Behind the wall on the left of the picture is a mansion now occupied by the Turkish Embassy.

If you continue along the Rue Raynouard you arrive at La Maison de Radio France, where there is a museum devoted to the history of radio and television. There are regular tours every day except Monday. The guides are French speaking, but even if you can't understand what they are saying it doesn't greatly matter for there is a lot to see if you happen to be technically minded. A visit to one of the television studios is included in the tour and while you are there you can obtain tickets for other audience shows.

An avid museum-goer could spend a week in the 16th arrondissement and still have barely scratched the surface of all there is to see. But if at the end of the day you emerge from La Maison de Radio France feeling saturated by so much culture, and suffering from strained eyesight, you can always seek suitable aid for your jaded eyeballs at 2 Avenue Mozart (Sundays and Mondays excepted), where the Musée des Lunettes et Lorgnettes de Jadis has over three thousand monocles, spectacles and reading glasses on permanent display. Either that, or you could metaphorically drown your sorrows in the vaulted cellars of the Musée du Vin, situated somewhat inappropriately in the Rue des Eaux near the Passy Metro station.

What did the Gauls do in the year 200 BC which is still being done today, although on an infinitely larger scale? How many different ways are there of spelling Byrrh? The answer to these and many other questions can be found at No. 16 Rue de la Faisanderie. The door may well be shut when you arrive, but on a weekday if you ring the bell a buzzer will sound and you will be free to enter the Musée de la Contrefaçon.

Inside is a collection of counterfeit labels and other objects. If wine in the year 200 BC wasn't always all that it was cracked up to be, today it is the manufacturers of perfume, spirits, apéritifs and chic, initialled luggage who suffer most. There are more ways of spelling Byrrh and Pernod on a label than one would have thought possible, and falsifiers trade on the fact that people tend to read what they expect to read.

Perhaps the unkindest cut of all is the fact that the building which houses the collection purports to be an eighteenth-century town house, but was in fact built in 1900. Altogether, though, a fascinating diversion if you happen to be en route to Rue Louis-Bouilly and the Musée Marmottan.

The Marmottan Museum (closed Mondays) contains a fine collection of Impressionist paintings – the best in Paris after the Musée d'Orsay. It began life in 1932 when the art historian Paul Marmottan bequeathed the house and his collection of paintings to the Institut de France. In 1950 a further legacy included Monet's 'Impression, Soleil Levant', from which the Impressionist Movement derived its name. But it was in 1971 that the museum gained its greatest treasures, when Michel Monet bequeathed sixty-five of his father's works, including his studies of light on the river Thames in London, and many paintings of the waterlilies in the lake at Giverny.

The bequest also included works by some of Monet's friends, including Morisot, Renoir, Jonkind and Sisley, all of which are housed in a specially constructed underground gallery along with displays of personal items relating to Monet himself.

The museum is pleasantly small and civilized and being off the beaten track is seldom as crowded as the larger ones in central Paris, so that it is possible to study the paintings at one's leisure, or simply sit and gaze. If it does nothing else it will make you long to visit Monet's old home at Giverny – a very good day's outing if you feel like a breath of country air.

At this point any architects might like to pay a visit to the Villa la Roche at 8 Square du Docteur Blanche. Designed by Le Corbusier in 1923, it now houses examples of his work as a painter and sculptor and has a large library containing microfilm of his architectural designs. (Closed week-ends and in August)

The 16th arrondissement also boasts several *maisons de passe* – discreet hotels where you can take a room in style for an hour or so. One, The Villa Caroline, at 85 Rue de la Pompe, has ten such rooms where you can take your ease on a mock-fur covered bed behind padded doors and enjoy a cold meal accompanied by a bottle of champagne. But if you want to be accompanied by anything more you will have to make your own arrangements.

If you are made of sterner stuff and long for a breath of fresh air, the Bois de Boulogne is but a stone's throw away. Strictly speaking it isn't part of the 16th, but it's near enough not to be too much of a cheat. With its lakes and its flower-gardens, its children's park and its race-courses, it has something for everyone and more than makes up for the comparative lack of parks in central Paris.

If you enter it by the Porte de la Muette, you are faced by the Lac Inférieur, where boats can be hired. There is also a ferry to the islands.

To the left is the Auteuil race-course, and beyond that the Fleuriste Municipal, where plants and flowers are grown for other Paris parks and for use on official occasions. The formal gardens, hothouses, and arboretum are well worth a visit. In late April azaleas are on display and in October chrysanthemums.

Nearby, in the car park of the Hôpital Amboise Paré, bicycles can be hired. (The Bois de Boulogne is full of cycle tracks.)

Whichever way you choose to travel, strolling along with an independent air, or on two wheels, if you carry on round the outside in a clockwise direction you come to the Longchamp race-course alongside the Seine and beyond that, past the Grande Cascade, is the Bagatelle. Once the home of the Hertfords, the château itself is no longer open to the public, but in its time it housed what is now known as the Wallace Collection in London. Sir Richard Wallace was also responsible for many of Paris's fountains.

Nowadays, the Bagatelle is famous for its gardens. In May there is a display of iris in the walled garden, and in June there are roses and water-lilies. But it is a garden for all seasons, with shrubberies and an orangery. There is also a good small restaurant which serves wine and snacks, but get there early on a busy day.

For a grander meal you need to go to the Pré Catalan in the centre of the park, where there is a restaurant by that name, also the largest tree in Paris – a copper beech whose branches cover an area of nearly 600 square yards – and a 'Shakespeare Garden', planted with every flower and herb mentioned in his plays.

North of the Pré Catalan, beyond two small lakes, is the Musée National des Arts et Traditions Populaires (closed Tuesdays and some holidays), which is full of things to do with French rural life prior to the Industrial Revolution, and where there are lots of working models.

But for children and the young in heart, the big attraction in the Bois de Boulogne is undoubtedly the Jardin D'Acclimatation, where there are all manner of ways of passing the time and of spending the francs. Radio-controlled model boats and cars, amusement arcades, a maze and hall of mirrors (the maze is the best value of all – it takes some children an age to find their way out, although it can end in tears), puppet shows, donkey and elephant rides, a cycling area where children can learn the rules of the road under the stern eye of a gendarme armed with a Tannoy, a museum of herbs, a giant dolls' house, a small zoo where guinea-pigs live in state alongside bears and other animals, a farmyard, miniature golf, places to eat, a giant helter-skelter, carousels, boat rides on an 'enchanted river', and a magnificent play area with giant climbing frames, swings galore and sandpits.

At the end of the day – when you are feeling totally worn out, make sure you have enough francs left to take the miniature train back to the Porte Maillot entrance gates. As you cross the Rue des Sablons a gendarme will hold up the traffic, and never before will a train ride have seemed so good or so worthwhile.

123 Rue Lauriston
Tel: 47.27.63.17
Cards: AE, CB, DC
Closed: Saturday,
Sunday, August, one
week at Christmas
Nearest Metro:
Trocadéro (6, 9)
Map ref: 1

Every so often you come across a restaurant where you immediately feel at home. There is a certain warmth about it, and as the waiter pulls aside one of the tables lining the walls and you squeeze through the gap in order to take your seat, a sense of *déjà vu* creeps over you.

Paul Chêne is one such establishment; the huge flower arrangement on the bar counter, the machine for slicing ham alongside it; the red plush seats and the snow white table-cloths, all add up to the kind of restaurant you find dotted about all over France. Solid, professional, totally reliable, filled with serious diners who discuss their choice of food knowledgeably with the waiter, knowing they will seldom be disappointed. Awarded a star by *Michelin* and a 'laurel' by *Gault-Millau* for his old 'regional recipes', which are of the south of France, Monsieur Chêne offers *boudin de campagne, poule au pot Henri IV, brandade* (creamed salt cod), *carré d'agneau, cassoulet* and the like, which are authentic, yet with subtle overtones which raise them to even greater heights and are the mark of a master chef who cares. Other dishes tried and heartily approved of are the escargots (delicious, but others say the smell of garlic lasts for days afterwards!), *soupe aux moules*, and apple fritters with currant jelly.

There is a good and interesting wine list, which includes both the great and the small; something for all tastes and pockets.

A classic restaurant which you leave wanting to return.

28 Rue Duret
Tel: 45.00.17.67
Cards: VISA
Closed: Saturday,
Sunday, beginning of
January
Nearest Metro:
Argentine (1)
Map ref: 2

Most French restaurants seem to boast some kind of idiosyncratic addition to their arrangements, be it an illuminated duck if the owner hails from the south-west, or the offering of wine in a giant wooden sabot if the cuisine is from, say, the Auvergne. Guy Savoy's contribution to the scene is a revolving door which doesn't look like one. It separates the regulars from the newcomers, endowing the former with a feeling of quiet superiority as they listen to the goings-on outside before the latter discover the secret. But once inside the elegant green and beige dining room all is quickly forgiven. The service is prompt, but never hurried, even if you happen to be dining early and the table is needed for a later sitting.

It is hard to sum up the food, for it is neither *haute cuisine* nor the extremes of *nouvelle*, more a happy marriage of the two. Monsieur Savoy is one of those chefs who is forever experimenting with what is available and takes his fancy on the day. Inspired is probably the best word to describe it; *escargots* with ravioli, or white cabbage with caviar (said to be one of Mr Gorbachev's favourite dishes, as well it might be).

There are two fixed-price menus – *le menu du marché* and *le menu prestige*, either of which is an excellent way of getting the measure of the food. There is an extremely good wine list, and, what is perhaps equally important, an unusually caring, knowledgeable and helpful young *sommelier*, whose advice is always worth taking, even if it does raise the bill a franc or two.

You will definitely need to book, often several days in advance – even when Monsieur Savoy is away tending to the needs of his other restaurant in Connecticut. Not the cheapest way of spending an evening, but one of the least regretful.

17e ARRONDISSEMENT

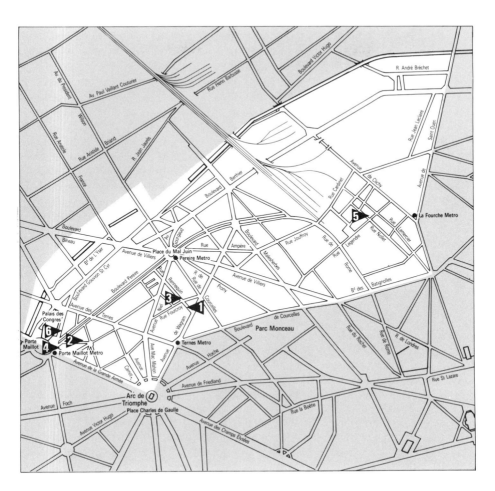

1. Chez la Mère Michel
2. La Coquille
3. Michel Rostang
4. Le Congrès
5. Chez Gorisse
6. La Grosse Tartine

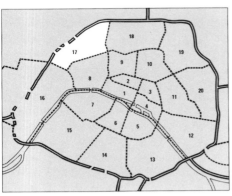

The vast complex known as the Centre International de Paris, or more familiarly as the Palais des Congrès, stands alongside the *Périphérique* at Porte Maillot, part of a long line of landmarks which begins at the Palais du Louvre, runs on through the Tuileries up the Champs Elysées, through the Arc-de-Triomphe, and on up the Avenues de la Grande Armée and Charles de Gaulle to La Défense, the futuristic sky-scraper development on the outskirts of Paris.

The Palais des Congrès.

The Palais des Congrès is a self-sufficient island set in a sea of converging *avenues* and *boulevards* along which traffic surges day and night. It is the home of the Paris Symphony Orchestra and boasts a dual-purpose hall for concerts and conferences which seats some 4,300 people, numerous suites, offices and smaller halls, four cinemas, two discotheques, around eighty boutiques arranged on two circular floors one above the other, and the 1,000-room Concorde La Fayette Hotel (parking for 1,500 cars). The Palais des Congrès is also a stopping point for Air France buses arriving from Charles de Gaulle airport at Roissy, and for those who happen to be attending a conference at the centre, the view from the Plein Ciel bar on the thirty-second floor of the Concorde La Fayette, although not to be despised, is probably all they will ever see of Paris.

Not that their efforts would be greatly rewarded if they decided to brave the traffic and explore their immediate surroundings. Apart from some good late-night jazz presented by Moustache in the Bar Lionel Hampton at the nearby Meridien Hotel in Boulevard Gouvion (from 22.00 onwards; the bar is in the patio area and admission is free, but there is a minimum charge for drinks) the 17th arrondissement is not what one might call a key tourist area.

Here and there, however, there are little pockets of civilization, past and present.

The Musée Jean-Jacques Henner at 43 Avenue de Villiers is one (closed mornings and on Mondays). It contains drawings and portraits by the Alsatian artist who achieved fame in the late 1800s, even if Degas did call him 'a two-bit Leonardo' and accused him of smoking too much while he did his somewhat hazy portraits.

If nothing else, the visit will take you to the most rewarding part of the 17th, the quartier Batignolles, an area which gave its name to a school of impressionist painters headed by Manet.

The Rue Lévis, leading from the junction of the Avenue de Villiers and Boulevard de Courcelles, is the scene on Saturdays of a thriving street market, and if you turn right into the Rue Legendre you come to the Eglise Ste Marie des Batignoles, behind which lies the Square de Batignoles. It is more of a park than a square, a quiet and peaceful backwater with a duck pond and winding gravel paths edged with low, cast-iron fencing shaped like interwoven twigs in a way that could only be French. Perhaps they were designed by an ancestor of the man who created the plastic 'twigs' for the besoms now used by Paris street cleaners.

Square de Batignoles.

5 Rue Rennequin
Tel: 47.63.59.80 or
47.63.94.14
Cards: VISA
Closed: Saturday,
Sunday, holidays and
August
Nearest Metro: Ternes
(2)
Map ref: 1

Chez la Mère Michel was established in the early thirties by Madame Michel, who won fame and a star in the *Michelin Guide* (which it still has) for her *beurre blanc Nantais* – with pike, but also with many other kinds of fish. Today the tradition is being carried on by Monsieur Gaillard, and the printed menu remains relatively unchanged. There are a few daily additions, but basically they still do what they do best: to start, either an excellent *terrine aux foies de volaille* or smoked eel; for the main course, fish with *beurre blanc*, or *poulet Mère Michel* – chicken with tarragon flavoured stuffing, browned and flamed in Armagnac, then roasted and served with a cream and madeira sauce – or baked ham with hazelnuts; and to end with, a choice of exceptionally good *omelettes soufflées*. The wine list is good on simple white wines, and despite what some guide-books might say, there is also a fair selection of reasonably priced clarets.

The restaurant is small and it is necessary to book. To enter it is like visiting someone's home. The welcome is warm and you are ushered to your seat by a Madame who has a pleasing eye for symmetry when it comes to laying the table; the silver bread baskets are continually being brought into line and the wine buckets know their place. Men tend to get served first. Monsieur comes in from time to time to help out and see how things are going in the outside world. Between visits satisfactory cooking noises can be heard emerging from the kitchen.

Connoisseurs of period French restaurants will like the lampshades, and a burglar in need of a quick pick-me-up might search all night for some ice without thinking of looking inside the giant bottle of White Lady which stands on the bar counter, and which parts in the middle. A reasonable bill at the end.

6 Rue Débarcadère
Tel: 45.74.25.95
Cards: VISA, EC
Closed: Sunday,
Monday, August, 24
December–1 January
Nearest Metro: Port
Maillot (1)
Map ref: 2

Each time I've been to *La Coquille* I have chosen exactly the same meal: *coquille St Jacques au naturel* (available from October to May, and one of the recommendations under the starred entry in *Michelin*); followed by *boudin noir*, served with apple and potatoes (a giant-size portion and probably as good as any you are likely to find, although the last time I was there a knowledgeable French diner at the next table was confiding to his friend that it was the second best in Paris – the very best, according to him, were to be found at the *Cochon d'Or* in the 19th arrondissement); and to end with, another *Michelin* recommendation – *soufflé au praslin de noisettes* (a popular choice if the number coming out of the kitchen towards the end of the evening is anything to go by).

But that's the way it is with some restaurants; taste buds suddenly send out urgent messages and you find yourself going back again and again for the same meal. Be that as it may, they are reputed to be good at game in season, liver with bacon, *fricassée* of chicken with cream and *morelles*, and *sole aux nouilles fraîches*. All good old-fashioned reasons for going back.

Old-fashioned also applies to the warmth of the welcome, the prompt and friendly service, and the ambience. Note the enormous lampshades hanging from the ceiling – of a size which wouldn't look out of place at Versailles, the mixture of fresh and artificial flowers on each table, the large bowl of artificial tulips, each head of which is internally illuminated, and the umbrella stand used to store *baguettes*.

There is a long wine list, packed with good things and very strong on Bordeaux. *Amuse-gueules* come with apéritif, and chocolates with the coffee, so no one goes away hungry. Perish the thought!

If you happen to be staying in the area on a first visit to Paris *La Coquille* is a very good introduction to what it's all about. If not, it's well worth a journey.

20 Rue Rennequin
Tel: 47.63.40.77
Cards: VISA
Closed: Saturday lunch,
Sunday, holidays, 25
July–25 August, Saturday
evenings April–September
Nearest Metro: Ternes
(2) or Pereire (3)
Map ref: 3

The dog leaning against the wall of Michel Rostang's restaurant has either been left there by his gourmet master, in which case he probably has a long wait ahead of him, or he knows a thing or two about food, which is why his tongue is hanging out. A few steps away from *Mère Michel*, but already possessed of a second *Michelin* star and heading, one feels, for a possible third, Monsieur Rostang perpetuates a family culinary tradition begun by his father in Antibes, and is more than making up for the latter's recent slight fall from grace.

First time visitors would do well to contemplate the *menu dégustation*, of which there is a choice of two, for they contain many specialities including incredibly light ravioli filled with fresh goat cheese and served in a chicken broth, than which there is no better way to begin a meal which will be *nouvelle cuisine* at its best; that is to say classic dishes, many – like the ravioli, from Monsieur Rostang's home region, the Savoie – which have been simplified without in any way losing the authentic flavour. Try, too, the *poulette de Bresse en pot-au-feu*, the *canette au sang* – pressed roast duck – or the *fricassée de soles*. Inspired cooking which is hard to fault.

Bread comes from a nearby branch of Monsieur Pain, and the wine list includes some superb red and white Beaucastel Châteauneuf-du-Pape. At lunch-time there is a cheaper fixed-price menu.

Monsieur Rostang and his wife are both much in evidence, greeting guests, offering advice and generally enjoying the fruits of their well-deserved success. It is an elegant restaurant and not over-large, therefore booking is essential, often a week or more in advance, but it will be well worth the trouble.

Le Congrès. 80 Avenue de la Grande-Armée. **Tel:** 45.74.17.24. **Cards:** AE, DC, EC, VISA. **Closed:** Open every day until 01.30. **Nearest Metro:** Porte Maillot (1). **Map ref:** 4.

Close to the Porte Maillot airport coach stop and its associated hotels, and therefore geared to that kind of trade. Always busy, and you may have to queue at peak times, but very good value if you fancy charcoal-grilled steak, fish, or oysters all the year round. A good introduction to eating in Paris if you have never been before, and probably the best value in the area.

Chez Gorisse. 84 Rue Nollet. **Tel:** 46.27.43.05. **Cards:** AE, VISA. **Closed:** Sunday, Monday lunch, August. **Nearest Metro:** La Fourche (13). **Map ref:** 5.

Situated in an out-of-the way, working-class area of the 17th, *Chez Gorisse* is the kind of bistro which should be preserved as a National Monument. In England you wouldn't give the outside a second look, knowing that inside it would almost certainly be grubby and empty. But this is France, and you will definitely need to book. Locals pay it the compliment of dressing up to eat there and then once seated they immediately remove their jackets so that they can get down to the serious business of eating hot *saucisson*, rabbit in mustard, *pot-au-feu*, or other dishes of the day. It has had several owners in recent years, but all carry on the tradition established years ago by Madame Gorisse. Excellent value.

La Grosse Tartine. 91 Boulevard Gouvion-Saint-Cyr. **Tel:** 45.74.02.77. **Cards:** AE, CB, DC. **Closed:** Sunday, Monday evening, Tuesday evening, three weeks in August. **Nearest Metro:** Porte Maillot (1). **Map ref:** 6.

Opposite the Palais des Congrès, *La Grosse Tartine* offers simple, unchanging fare of salads, *charcuteries*, and desserts, together with a *plat-du-jour* like *pot-au-feu*, at a very reasonable price. It belongs to the wine merchant next door, so there is always something interesting to drink, either in quarter or half-litre *pichets*, or by the bottle. There is a small courtyard where you can eat during the summer.

18e ARRONDISSEMENT

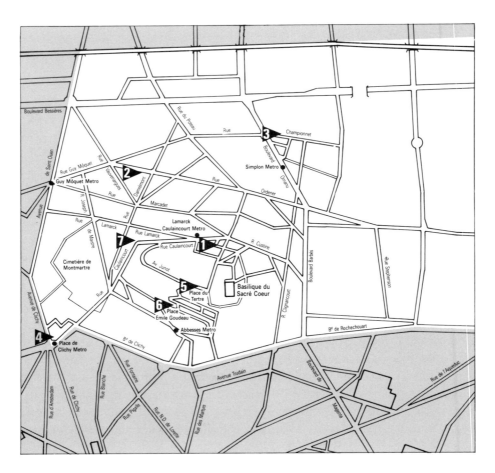

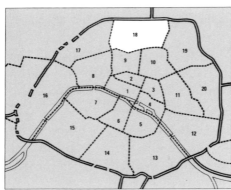

1. Beauvilliers
2. Chez Frezet
3. Marie-Louise
4. Le Wepler
5. Mère Catherine
6. Relais de la Butte
7. Clodenis

These two ladies enjoying the morning sunshine in the Place des Abbesses represent the 'lived-in', residential side of the 18th arrondissement. The entrance to the station in the background is a good example of the *fin de siècle* architecture of Monsieur Guimard, who was responsible for the exterior design of most of the original Metro stations.

There was a time when many of these stylish entrances were replaced in the name of progress. Some even found themselves

enjoying a new lease of life in unexpected surroundings, like the one in the Museum of Modern Art in New York. However, when *art nouveau* became fashionable again preservation orders were served on those that were left, and although one or two – like the one at Abbesses – are reproductions, there are still some forty or so of the originals remaining, notably on Line 2.

The 18th arrondissement ought to have the cleanest gutters in all Paris, if only because each day water is pumped out of the ground at the highest points and makes its inevitable way downhill, carrying all before it. Pigeons and sparrows use it for their morning ablutions and from time to time men in overalls appear in order to divert it with pieces of old carpet tied up with string.

The French may have embraced the technological age with both arms, but they are a very practical people at heart and no one has yet come up with a better system, so why change it? The same men also wield besoms made of imitation plastic twigs, doubtless for an equally good reason.

If Montmartre doesn't have the best gutters it is not the fault of the street cleaners, or their mobile colleagues (Caninettes) – uniformed men on motor cycles who patrol the pavements looking for visiting cards left by local *chiens* – Montmartre seems to have more than its fair share of Paris's estimated daily twenty tons – whisking them away by means of a revolving brush or suction tube.

The fact is that the foothills, which lie along the Boulevards Clichy, Rochechouart and de la Chapelle, embrace a great deal of all that is worst in human nature, and the inhabitants are not exactly noted either for their cleanliness or their sensitivity.

Outside each clip joint touts await the arrival of the next tourist bus; sex shops abound; porno movie houses vie with each other in their efforts to give 'best' value for money; girls lurk in doorways and on the pavements, singly and in intimidating groups, for most of the twenty-four hours in each and every day; the further east you go along the Boulevard de la Chapelle, scene of much violence when the North African troubles were at their height, the shriller the voices and the riper the language.

It is all a bit like the Casbah in its prime, and like the Casbah it is best seen at night, when it has a certain 'romance'; by day it is merely sordid and best left behind you. Either take the Metro to Pigalle and catch the little Montmartrobus, which leaves every ten minutes from seven-thirty in the morning onwards, winding its way up to the Place du Tertre and beyond, or disembark at Anvers and push your way on foot up the crowded Rue Steinkerque until you come to the Square Willette, which lies immediately below the Sacré-Coeur. Here you can either climb the three hundred and thirty-five steps to the top or, for the price of a Metro ticket, take the Funicular – worth every centime for the view across Paris from the top – and a visit to the Sacré-Coeur itself. Despite its sugar-icing architecture, the latter is still a moving experience within.

To the west of the Sacré-Coeur lies the Place du Tertre. At the height of summer it is packed with tourists, most of whom seem to be either having their portrait painted or are posing for shadowgraphs, and you may well feel at this point that you have 'done' Montmartre – or that Montmartre has 'done' you. This would be a pity, because all around, and particularly to the North and West, there is a great deal to see and enjoy. Pictorially – apart from all the parked cars – it is still full of the kind of views that Utrillo painted when he lived at 12 Rue Cortot.

Until 1860, when it officially became part of Paris, Montmartre was just a village. The Butte Montmarte stands 423 feet above sea level and was a difficult area to develop, for it was the site of an old plaster-of-Paris quarry and riddled with underground passages, many of which were used by the Resistance movement during the last war.

In its heyday it was alive with windmills used for grinding flour. The most famous, the Moulin de la Galette, was immortalized by Renoir after it became a dance hall. Signs will lead you from the Place du Tertre to a waxworks museum at 11 Rue Poulbot where many famous characters who made Montmartre their home – Renoir, Liszt, Chopin, Toulouse-Lautrec – are depicted.

To the south-west is the Place Emile Goudeau, site of the Bateau-Lavoir, where Picasso, Gris, Modigliani and the poet Max Jacob – who died in a concentration camp – once lived and worked in poverty. It was here that Picasso painted Les Demoiselles d'Avignon – the start of the Cubist movement – maintaining that he was never so happy as he was then, living with Fernande Olivier, shopping at the nearby Cochon Rose and sharing the single water tap with his friends. Sadly the *atelier* was destroyed by fire in 1970 just as it was about to be restored and turned into a museum.

North-west of the Place du Tertre, down the Rue des Saules, is the old *Lapin Agile* cabaret, which manages to retain a surprisingly authentic feel despite all the tourists, and where *eau de vie* with a cherry is still the traditional drink.

On the opposite corner lies the only vineyard in Paris, producing, as might be expected, a thinnish white wine, which is nevertheless a source of much pride and celebration at harvest time on the first Saturday in October every year.

In the bottom left-hand corner of the arrondissement is the Cimetière de Montmartre; a very literary cemetery containing the tombs of Mme Récamier, Stendhal, Dumas, Gautier, the Goncourts, Emile Zola and Sacha Guitry. Close by, at 22 Rue Tourlaque, a new artist's colony has arisen.

To the far north, beyond the *Périphérique* at Porte de Clignancourt, is the famous flea market – open on Saturdays, Sundays and Mondays – which is worth at least one visit, although bargains are few and far between and it is as well to keep a tight hold on your wallet.

If climbing up and down all the steps has worn you out and you feel like a good, long rest, there is a small cinema in the Rue Tholoze which has a complete change of programme daily, with separate showings at 3.00, 5.00, 7.00, and 9.00, and has comfortable armchair seating. Or, you can make one last sortie up the Hill of Martyrs past the one remaining windmill–now part of a luxury block of apartments – to the Rue Guardes.

A little way along on the left is the entrance to some gardens, part of which has been laid out as an official *boules* station for the 'Boules de Montmartre'. The *boules* area itself is *interdit* to the general public, and it would be a brave man indeed who entered uninvited, but you can spend a pleasant half-hour or so sitting on a bench outside watching the same old players having exactly the same arguments about the finer points of the game as they must have done every other afternoon of the year, adding an air of permanence to the scene.

52 Rue Lamarck
Tel: 42.54.54.42
Cards: VISA
Closed: Sunday,
Monday (lunch), first two
weeks in September
Nearest Metro:
Lamarck-Caulaincourt
(12)
Map ref: 1

Set in a converted bakery on the northern slopes of Montmartre, the *Beauvilliers* is one of the most stylish and tasteful of restaurants. Enormous vases of flowers abound, the walls are decorated with a profusion of paintings and engravings, and the table settings are equally beautiful. All of which adds up to the prospect of a large bill even before you start to eat; a feeling which is confirmed when you are offered the house apéritif of champagne and *fraise*. At something like seventy francs for two it's not a place to visit every night of the week. But the service is first rate, friendly and knowledgeable, and the food thoroughly deserves the three 'toques' awarded it by *Gault-Millau*. (One star in *Michelin*.)

The menu is changed every week, so it would be pointless to mention individual dishes, except to say that the cheese, when it arrives, is presented on two separate boards – one for goat's milk and the other for cow's and both are seductively and irresistibly laid out in a way which you could only encounter in France.

The wine list contains a lot of less familiar names as well as those from the higher echelons. Many of them, as is so often the case in France, are younger than we would normally drink, but there are some older wines at a price.

In summer there is a terrace which looks out over the rooftops of buildings lower down the hill. Strangely for a restaurant created with such exquisite taste, there is taped music in the background. Once, very pianissimo, we distinctly recognized the 'Lambeth Walk'! The coffee comes with the biggest selection of sugar you are ever likely to encounter. You leave having spent quite a lot of money, but with no regrets, for it will have been worth every franc.

181 Rue Ordener
Tel: 46.06.64.20
Cards: AE, VISA
Closed: Saturday,
Sunday, during February,
school holidays, August
Nearest Metro: Guy
Moquet (13)
Map ref: 2

You enter this restaurant past a display of shellfish and through a tiny bar with a couple of tables, wondering why you bothered to book beforehand (which is usually necessary). Then, having established the fact that you have indeed reserved a table, as like as not you will find yourself being shooed down a corridor by a formidable but kindly waitress of the old school, who utters cries of '*Avancez*' as she relieves you of your coat and ushers you into the dining-room proper in one sweeping movement.

There you will find yourself inside a good, old-fashioned restaurant which serves, as it has done year in, year out, unvaryingly reliable food to regulars who know a good meal when they see one. Each day has its speciality, so you always know where you stand, and so presumably does the chef. Monday and Thursday – *bouillabaisse*; Tuesday – *cassoulet*; Wednesday – fish stew; Friday – *gigot en feuilleté*. But there are many other good things permanently on the menu. For example, *rosette de Lyon* (thinly sliced sausage) and sea bass flamed in pernod.

The fish is always good and fresh, as only Paris fish can be. The waitresses are incredibly efficient, with not a wasted movement. On crowded evenings it is both a pleasure and an object lesson to watch them gather speed as the pace builds up, although if you happen to get the formidable one who took your coats you will find she has decided views on what goes with what. Dallying over the menu gives rise to ill-suppressed sucking noises, and *frites* do *not* go with everything.

There is an adequate wine list designed more for those who consider it a natural accompaniment to a meal rather than have any great interest in its gastronomic possibilities. Some old Armagnacs are generously served and the bottle is left on the table! Being a family restaurant catering mainly for local residents, it is closed during school holidays. Very good value.

52 Rue Championnet
Tel: 46.06.86.55
Cards: DC, VISA
Closed: Sunday,
Monday, Fête days, end
of July until the
beginning of September
Nearest Metro:
Simplon (4)
Map ref: 3

Marie-Louise is one of those restaurants that feels as though it has been there for ever, and will go on being there for ever, its décor unchanged along with the menu and the hunting prints on the wall. It is a classic, small French restaurant and it represents a way of life. If you want to escape the worst excesses of *nouvelle cuisine* this is the place to come. No goings-on of that kind here. You can see, and often hear, Monsieur Coillot doing the cooking out back. Madame Coillot is out front.

For many years they had a star in the *Guide Michelin*, and then a few years ago Monsieur Coillot lost it. Perhaps the Inspector had the same *clafoutis* I ordered one evening – normally good, but for once terrible. A slight air of gloom descended on the restaurant, as if the system had received a great shock and had lost the will to recover. But just lately they seem to be fighting back. The hand-written list of the day's specialities is longer; the wine list has improved enormously and they have even started to put the year against some of them. Who knows, perhaps their star is in the ascendancy again? In any event, the clientèle has remained faithful, secure in the knowledge that they are on safe ground.

I have eaten there more than in any other French restaurant and have never come away feeling less than happy and replete. The first courses are mainly classically simple – *salade de concombre*, *salade de tomates*, etc., but the helpings are more than generous, so be warned! The last time I was there I was served a delicious *carré d'agneau*, as tender as it could possibly be and cooked to perfection, served with *haricots flageolets au beurre* and with the pots left on the table to be finished up. Another speciality is *poularde Marie-Louise* and there are delicious *tartelettes* to follow.

A Kir to begin with, Perrier, a bottle of 1977 Cos d'Etournel, a delicious meal and coffee to end with – all at a very reasonable price. What more could you want?

Le Wepler (M. Bessière). 14 Place Clichy.   **Tel:** 45.22.53.24.   **Cards:** AE, DC, EC, VISA.
Closed: during August.   **Nearest Metro:** Place Clichy (2, 13).   **Map ref:** 4.

Le Wepler is one of those giant, bustling Paris restaurants specializing in sea-food – oysters, prawns, langoustines, sea urchins and mussels; anything, in fact, which moves on the sea bed. Open until two in the morning. Thoroughly reliable. Reasonably priced. Always busy.

Mère Catherine. 6 Place du Tertre. **Tel:** 46.06.32.69. **Cards:** AE. DC. EC. **Nearest Metro:** Abbesses. **Map ref:** 5.

If you must eat in the Place du Tertre, then *Mère Catherine* is probably a better bet than most. It has been serving coq au vin since 1793, when it was a meeting place for huntsmen, so they should have got it right by now. Prices are moderate.

Relais de la Butte. 12 Rue Ravignon.   **Tel:** 46.06.16.18.   **Cards:** AE, DC.   **Closed:** Monday and during August.   **Nearest Metro:** Abbesses (12).   **Map ref:** 6.

Another of those Montmartre restaurants that once enjoyed a star in the *Guide Michelin*. Included for partly sentimental reasons. It was the first Paris restaurant I ever ate in and I still have a 'Grand Marnier' corkscrew one of the waiters gave me. In those days when you ordered garlic soup there was a great pounding noise from the kitchen upstairs and you could practically see the fumes coming down the stairs. Over the last few years there have been several changes of ownership and standards have fallen and risen again accordingly. The last time we went it was being run by an ex-captain of a *bateau-mouche*, Monsieur Vogel, who seemed to be coping well with the passengers. Prices are very reasonable and, being situated on the corner of the Place Emile Goudeau, opposite the Bateau-Lavoir, it is off the main night-time tourist tracks.

Clodenis. 57 Rue Caulaincourt.   **Tel:** 46.06.20.26.   **Cards:** AE, DC, EC, VISA.   **Closed:**
. Sunday.   **Nearest Metro:** Lamarck-Caulaincourt (12).   **Map ref:** 7.

Less elegant and more bistro-ish than *Beauvilliers*, but one tends to think of the two in the same breath. The menu is short and the cooking very much *nouvelle cuisine*.

19e ARRONDISSEMENT

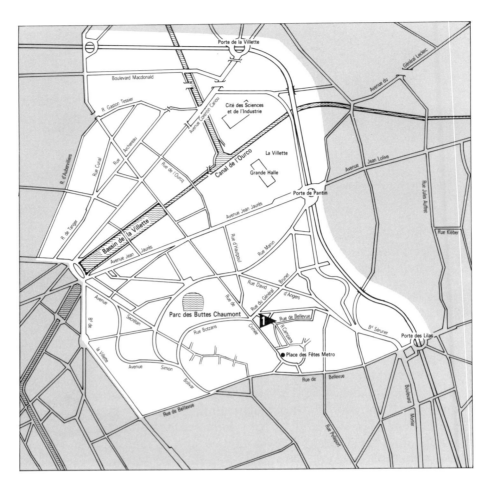

1. Le Petit Pré

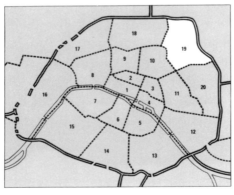

'What on earth,' this dog on the right seems to be saying, 'are *you* doing here?' The idea of anyone actually visiting the 19th arrondissement for pleasure seems to be totally beyond his comprehension, and when you take a look around you can see that in many respects he has a point.

     Perhaps he had never been taken for 'walkies' in the Parc des Buttes-Chaumont; the only park in Paris where you can actually tread

on the grass without incurring the wrath and whistle-blowing of any passing *gendarme*.

Baron Haussman built the park on the site of some old gypsum mines at the request of Napoleon III. The name Chaumont means 'bare mountain' and in the old days there was an execution site nearby – the *Gibet de Montfaucon*. François Villon, songwriter and member of a gang called *Les Coquillards* – the Shellfish Brothers – wrote about it.

There is a lake, fed by the Canal St Martin, and a rocky island with a waterfall, grottoes and a Roman-style temple (pictured overleaf). The island rises to 150 feet and you don't need a clear day to see across to Montmartre. On sunny days it makes a good excursion and is a pleasant change from the formality of the Tuileries or the Luxembourg Gardens. You can even walk on the grass.

If you spend the morning strolling round the park and working up an appetite, you could do worse than eat at Le Pavillon du Lac, where there is a lovely view and country style food to match the mood.

Temple in the Parc Buttes-Chaumont.

If your tastes run to the scientific rather than the bucolic, then north of the Buttes-Chaumont, on the site of the old La Villette meat market, is a project so vast that even the French, accustomed to buildings on a grand scale, gaze at it in awe.

The core of the complex involves a one million franc building which was to have been the most advanced slaughterhouse in Europe, but became obsolete before it even opened. For a while its empty shell remained a pawn in the game of party politics, but now at a cost of a further four billion francs it has been transformed into the La Cité des

Sciences et de l'Industrie (Centre for Science and Industry) and will be the most advanced museum of its kind in the world, covering every aspect of science, from the exploration of the ocean bed, via a mock-up of a Nautilus submarine complete with robot diver who answers questions put to him by visitors, to a life-size model of a future space station and the infinity which lies beyond.

Between the two extremes are sections devoted to various aspects of human activity. There are games to be played, computers to operate, areas devoted to having fun with mathematics, others to the nature of life. In all of them the emphasis is on involvement and having fun whilst learning. For a child with an enquiring mind it is a must; the world-weary adult who thinks he has seen it all can only gaze in wonderment. He won't be allowed anywhere near the buttons.

Outside the Centre, the 6,433 triangles of polished stainless steel which go to make up the skin of this giant Géode, reflect not only the sky, but also an Impressionist-style picture of various other diversions on the thirty-five acre site: a Grande Halle for concerts and exhibitions, the 'Zenith' rock music hall, and various 'theme parks' containing restaurants, gardens, and a fabulous dragon whose protruding tongue makes a wonderful children's slide as it winds its way down a small hill.

Although the Géode may look as if it is floating on water, it is, in fact, very firmly anchored. It needs to be, for it contains the largest hemispheric projection screen in the world – over 10,000 square feet of it. Every hour, up to 350 spectators recline comfortably in the middle and are engulfed by laser images to the accompaniment of

La Patache *cruising on the canal St Martin.*

12,000 watts of sound. A unique, all-enveloping experience, particularly if you happen to catch a film like 'The Dream is Alive' – made during the course of several NASA missions into space. But if you suffer from dizziness or sensitive hearing, you may need to close your eyes from time to time, whilst letting go of the armrests on your chair in order to block your ears.

If the thought of all that concrete and stainless steel makes you long for a return to *La Belle Epoque*, then the most rewarding method of escape is to make the return trip to the centre of Paris by catamaran.

Every day at two o'clock between 1 April and 4 November (Mondays and public holidays excepted) *La Patache* leaves the Quai de la Loire in the Bassin de la Villette, and deposits you some three

hours later on the Quai Anatole-France on the left bank of the Seine opposite the Tuileries Gardens. (Conversely it sets out in the opposite direction at 09.00.)

You need to book in advance on 48.74.75.00; at week-ends well in advance and, if you want a seat near the front of the boat, as early as possible on other days. Names are called out from a nominal roll strictly in order of booking. The journey takes you through another world of ancient locks, wrought-iron bridges and a two kilometre long vaulted tunnel near the Bastille before it reaches the Seine. It is a world virtually unchanged since the turn of the century; fishermen line the banks and friendly waves are exchanged as they hold up their catch for all to see; attendants greet you at every stop; altogether it is a unique experience. (See also 10 Arr.) But be warned, the wooden seats can get very hard after three hours, so be prepared.

LE PETIT PRÉ.   M. VERGÈS.

1 Rue Bellevue
Tel: 42.08.92.62
Cards: None
Closed: Saturday,
Sunday, holidays, August
Nearest Metro: Place
de Fêtes (11)
Map ref: 1

You come out of the Metro station in the Place des Fêtes, with its bustling street market, walk a little way down the Rue Compans, and there in front of you stands *Le Petit Pré*, nestling in a little untouched corner of Belleville, and looking almost countrified by comparison with the surrounding apartment blocks.

Inside, the décor is suitably rustic, with beamed ceilings covered in brown material and copper pots and pans lining the walls. It is the kind of restaurant Monsieur Hulot would have enjoyed, if only because of the profusion of flowers, not all of which are real. One can almost picture his reaction on sniffing the ones that aren't.

Madame Jacqueline Vergès is chic, welcoming, and not at all put out when you explain that you are late because you went to the Rue de Belle*ville* first by mistake; clearly a not uncommon experience. You can repair the damage to your self-esteem over a Kir Royal which is served at your table in glasses ice-cold from the refrigerator.

Tried and approved are the Auvergne ham with green salad – which in France has an entirely different meaning to that in England, pigeon, *fricassée de lapereau* with pasta, *crêpes*, and chocolate mint *gâteau*. The bread is good, and there are tasty tit-bits before and after the meal. True, there are occasional lapses; the salad which accompanies the artichoke hearts, for example, has too many flavours for the sake of a little extra colour, but they are few and far between, so one hesitates to mention them when Monsieur Vergès arrives on the scene to enquire if you are happy. The answer is a definite '*oui*'.

Le Petit Pré is a favourite pasture for local businessmen at lunchtime, who must stagger back to their offices ready for sleep, having dined well from a menu of classic dishes, with innovative overtones, accompanied by excellent, reasonably priced wines from a very good, well-balanced list.

In the Avenue Jean Jaurès, near the old abbatoirs, between numbers 184 and 192, there is a row of good, traditional restaurants, all but one – *La Mer*, specializing in meat dishes. The others, *Au Boeuf Couronné*, *Dagorno*, *A la Ferme de la Villette* and *Au Cochon d'Or*, are all reliable, generous in their helpings, and probably can't wait for the completion of the complex in the old meat market across the road so that they can regain some of their old glory.

20ᵉ ARRONDISSEMENT

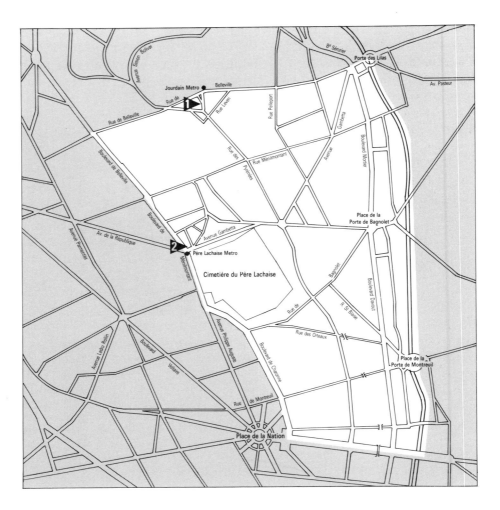

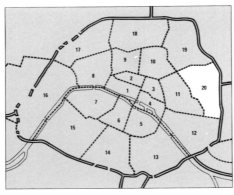

1. Relais des Pyrénées
2. Aux Becs Fins

The 20th arrondissement is being ripped apart by developers in the name of progress. The slums of yesterday have been raised to new heights and already buildings which must have seemed very grand and forward-thinking on the drawing board are being covered in graffiti by discontented occupants moved up in the world against their will.

Who knows what stories the walls of this little hotel in the Rue des Amandiers could tell if only they were able to talk? Tales of ships that passed in the night, of intrigues, of loneliness and passion, of travellers from foreign parts, of happiness shared and of lovers' tiffs ...

Soon they will have lost their chance, for like many another building in the area they will disappear beneath the bulldozer.

This is the area of the Quartiers Belleville and Menilmontant – once separated by vineyards and meadows – an area of artisans and small workshops, where in between rows of run-down, peeling two-storey houses you come across unexpected little country lanes and flower-filled gardens. It was an area made famous by the film *The Red Balloon*; where Edith Piaf was born in a doorway and grew up on the pavements, and where Maurice Chevalier began his career. It is a poor area – the eastern side of a city is always the poorest because the prevailing winds are from the west and would keep the smell away from richer folk – but those who knew it in the old days say that at Christmas the shops were full of food and other goodies which even the grander parts of Paris would have found it hard to match.

Belleville has suffered worst, and the windy hill on which it stands (and where *The Red Balloon* was filmed) is now littered with skyscraper apartment blocks. In many ways it has to be better; running hot and cold water and no more communal toilets, but it is very charmless and the neighbourly warmth which must once have bound it all together has gone; the only contact many of its inhabitants now have with the outside world is via their television sets. But that is a universal story.

This little blanchisserie *is also awaiting its fate. In its place there will be a high-rise apartment block and the inhabitants will all have their own washing-machine. But will they be any happier? It's*

impossible to say. Life in this part of the world has always been a matter of swings and roundabouts.

It is a part of Paris which doesn't figure in many tourist guides, but if you want a whiff of old Paris – the Paris of the nostalgic black and white postcards – go there soon. Choose a sunny day in spring or early summer when the flowers are out. Take the Metro to Belleville and explore the area to the south-east of the Boulevard Belleville, past Menilmontant Metro station and on as far as Père Lachaise. You will find tiny houses, leafy front gardens behind their railings and potted plants in their windows, alley-ways and narrow *impasses* which lead nowhere because there was nowhere to go. Here and there you will see little restaurants with paper tablecloths bearing bottles of *vin ordinaire*, occasionally with a tiled exterior – an indication that it was once a brothel in the days when the hillsides were alive with cabarets and open-air dance halls.

Look out for the Villa d'Ermitage, in a little lane off the Rue d'Ermitage; the Villa Faucher, off the Rue Piat, for a fine view of Paris; and the Rue du Télégraphe, where Monsieur Claude Chappe sent the first message by optical telegraph. The Cimetière de Belleville, at 419 feet, is the highest point in Paris, beating Montmartre by a metre; and further south, to the east of the Père Lachaise cemetery, is the church of Saint-Germain-de-Charonne, possibly the most rural churchyard in Paris, and the only one to have its own cemetery.

One part of the 20th arrondissement which remains sacred and inviolate to those who would plan its future is the Cimetière Père Lachaise.

The church of Saint-Germain-de-Charonne.

The cemetery is by far the largest in Paris and was named after Father de la Chaise, Jesuit priest and confessor to Louis XIV, whose country seat occupied the original site. After the Revolutionary Assembly banned the burying of dead within church grounds, Napoleon ordered the building of four new cemeteries outside the then walls of Paris, and the architect Brougniard was given the task of designing the Père Lachaise. He retained the rows of lime and chestnut trees from the old gardens, and took advantage of the hilly site by landscaping the rest with winding paths and more trees. Soon after it opened in 1804, in order to popularize it, a shrine was built for the famous twelfth-century lovers, Abélard and Héloïse, and their remains were moved from their original resting-place.

There are now around a million people buried in Père Lachaise. Beneath an assortment of tombs, mausoleums, temples and simple gravestones, Christians, Jews and Moslems rest alongside Hindus and Communists, their memory enshrined in every possible form of statuary. Angels and cherubs abound, as do nymphs in poses which leave little to the imagination. The list of famous people reads like a Who's Who of the world of arts, and to take full advantage of a visit a map is essential (it is possible to buy one at the gate when you go in).

Colette, Rossini, Baron Haussman, Cherubini, Corot, Molière, the Hugo family, Sarah Bernhardt, Marcel Proust, Balzac, Bizet, La Fontaine, Gertrude Stein, Daumier, Sir Richard Hertford-Wallace, benefactor of Paris, all attract their groups of worshippers. Modigliani, who died of consumption at the age of thirty-eight, shares a grave with his 'devoted companion' Jeanne Hebuterne – who jumped out of a window the day after. Chopin, Delacroix and Alfred de Musset, lovers of George Sand, are there, although, perhaps wisely, George Sand herself is buried elsewhere. Jim Morrison, leader of the rock group Doors, who died of an overdose of drugs in 1971, is much visited by his disciples, some of whom seem to be heading the same way, and there is always a small group around the tomb of Allan Kardec, founder of 'spiritual philosophy'; ladies reaching out to touch his statue on account of its supposed healing powers, or simply hoping to make contact with 'the other side'. Edith Piaf, who in life 'had no regrets', lies buried beneath a grave which never lacks flowers.

Others come to visit the *Mur des Fédérés* – the Federalists' Wall in the north-east corner. Scene of the Paris Commune's final stand on 28 May 1871, where 147 survivors were shot at dawn, it is still a place of pilgrimage for left-wing militants.

Nearby there is also a moving monument to the many Frenchmen who died in German concentration camps or as members of the Resistance during the last war.

In the northern corner there is a Moslem burial ground and not far away a *columbarium*, outside which row upon row of windowed compartments are filled with photographs, flowers and ashes of departed loved ones. Isadora Duncan is in one of the drawers. Nowadays you need to be rich or very famous to be buried in Père

Lachaise, but a numbered deposit box in the *columbarium* can still be bought for varying periods of time, including for ever.

The Cimetière Père Lachaise is a fascinating place to visit. Inhabited by ghosts of the past, little old ladies scurrying to and fro with their flowers, owls, young lovers, elderly *voyeurs*, families on outings, necrophiliacs, several hundred stray cats, and innumerable statues of the departed, it is also strangely romantic.

One wonders what this lady thinks of it all; clearly her mind is not on her book. Perhaps she is contemplating the fate of a near neighbour of hers, Oscar Wilde.

Sculpted by Epstein with all the weight of the world on his

shoulders, Wilde, who 'could resist everything except temptation', died in a sordid room in the Rue des Beaux-Arts – now a part of the chic and expensive L'Hôtel.

His private parts were broken off by two English ladies who took exception to their size, and for while they served as paper-weights in the cemetery office. The three foot long cat which is said to attack young girls after dark (who presumably shouldn't be in the cemetery anyway, since it closes at dusk) obviously hasn't suffered the same fate. One is tempted to paraphrase Wilde's immortal lines: 'To lose one parent may be regarded as a misfortune; to lose both looks like carelessness'.

1 Rue du Jourdain
Tel: 46.36.65.81
Cards: AE, DC, EC, VISA
Closed: Saturday, August
Nearest Metro: Jourdain (11)
Map ref: 1

Situated on the heights of Belleville, not far from the Cimetière de Belleville, the *Relais des Pyrénées* is relatively off the beaten track, but well worth a visit if you don't mind the journey or happen to be in the area, and is one of those restaurants which you leave discussing when you can go there next. Not that it is in any way sensational, but simply that everyone will have gone out of their way to make you feel at home without overwhelming you with *bonhomie*, either false or otherwise.

Monsieur Marty is a member of the *Maîtres Cuisiniers de France*, and his classical cooking reflects the area of the Pyrénées around Pau; *omelette pipérade, fois gras de canard, saumon au champagne, poulet Basquaise, cassoulet, confit d'oie* are amongst his specialities. *Garbure* – pork stew with vegetables and confit, virtually three dishes in one – perhaps not surprisingly requires two days' notice and as many days to recover, for portions are generous.

Madame Marty looks after the customers, assisted by knowledge-able waiters of the old school who look as if they have been there for as long as the skin of the old mountain lion who watches over them and is a feature of the otherwise sober décor.

The wine list is most impressive on clarets. There are very few at the cheaper end, but compared with many places the ones that are listed are moderately priced and include at the time of writing such goodies as a 1929 Croizet-Bages and a 1934 Mouton d'Armailhacq. Some good Côtes du Rhone and Burgundies, including a ten-year-old Cornas are listed, along with a few – a very few – *vins ordinaires*. All are served with equal love and care and interest. Sweets include various *soufflés, sorbets* and *clafoutis*.

A good place to be on a cold winter's evening.

44 Boulevard de
Ménilmontant
Tel: 47.97.51.52
Cards: AE, DC, VISA
Closed: Sunday lunch,
10–26 September
Nearest Metro: Père
Lachaise (2, 3)
Map ref: 2

If you happen to find yourself tired and hungry after visiting the Cimetière Père Lachaise, then help is at hand in the form of *Aux Becs Fins*, right outside the Metro station named after the cemetery. You should also visit it if only because one day it won't be there, for when the time comes for Mesdames Lefèbvre to hang up their aprons for the last time the restaurant whose fame has spread far and wide will be no more.

It is an entirely female, although in no way feminine establishment. The décor is rustic – wooden rakes hang from the ceiling (horizontally), ancient dressed puppets line the walls. The clientèle is for the most part French and local. There are two fixed-price menus – one with four courses including cheese and house wine, the other without the wine and a choice of cheese or sweet. Both are chalked on a blackboard which is left propped on a convenient chair while you reach a decision. The helpings are generous, the service efficient.

The premises are small, tables are in a long line down one wall and facing the bar, but there is a little closed-in terrace outside with several more tables, and an iron spiral staircase leads to an upper floor and another blackboard. A large bull-terrier watches over the proceedings with a non-committal air, until it comes to sampling the *terrines*, of which he clearly approves. No singing is allowed, but with Mesdames Lefèbvre on hand it would be a brave man who tried.

The wine list is long on weight if not on content, and for a restaurant where fish figures strongly on the menu there is a lack of white wines, although there is a passable Muscadet and a drinkable white Beaujolais. All are more reasonably priced than the food.

Useful Addresses and Telephone Numbers

Airways
Air France: 119 Avenue des Champs Elysées. Tel: 45.35.61.61 (Res.)
British Airways: 91 Avenue des Champs Elysées. Tel: 47.78.14.14
Pan Am: 1 Rue Scribe. Tel: 42.66.45.45
TWA: 101 Avenue des Champs Elysées. Tel: 47.23.54.33
Air Inter (Internal flights): 12 Rue de Castiglione. Tel: 42.60.36.46

American Express
11 Rue Scribe. Tel: 42.66.09.99
Open Monday – Friday 09.00–17.00, Saturday 09.00–12.00

Anything
Anything you need (within reason). A bridge partner, translators, stuffed animals – you name it.
Madame Service. 76 Rue Lemercier. Tel: 42.28.15.30

Baby-Sitters
(At any time, day or night, home or hotel)
Nurse Service. 33 Rue Fortuny. Tel: 46.22.26.22

Chemists
Look out for green and white neon cross. The *pharmacien* will be a highly qualified dispensing chemist and first-aid expert, only too pleased to offer his advice.

All night chemists:
Pharmacie des Champs Elysées. 84 Avenue des Champs Elysées. Tel: 45.62.02.41
Pharmacie Anglaise. 62 Avenue des Champs Elysées. Tel: 42.25.25.13
In other areas outside normal opening hours, look for lists on chemists' doors or ask at the local police station.

Embassies
United Kingdom. 35 Rue de Faubourg St Honoré. Tel: 42.66.91.42
United States. 2 Avenue Gabriel. Tel: 42.96.12.02

Emergencies
Police. Tel: 17
Fire. Tel: 18
Ambulance. Tel: 18 or 43.78.26.26
There are automatic call boxes at many main cross-roads for use in an emergency when the police or first aid are required.
For other emergencies after 19.00 hours try the *English Samaritan Services* who have a reputation for being very helpful. Tel: 47.23.80.80

USEFUL ADDRESSES AND TELEPHONE NUMBERS

Hospitals
British Hertford Hospital. 48 Rue de Villiers, Levallois-Perret. Tel: 47.58.13.12
American Hospital. 63 Boulevard Victor-Hugo, Neuilly. Tel: 47.47.53.00 They also have a dental clinic.
Both hospitals are about 5 miles from the centre of Paris.
Emergency Dentists. Tel: 43.37.51.00

Information
The *Office de Tourisme de Paris* at 127 Avenue des Champs Elysées provides hostesses between 09.00 and midnight to answer your queries. There is a Tourist Information Office in the Hotel de Ville, 29 Rue de Rivoli.

Lost property
Articles lost on the Metro or in buses are held for the first 48 hours at the terminus of the route concerned. After that, or in the case of articles lost elsewhere, try at the *Bureau des Objets Trouvés*, 36 Rue des Morillons. 15 arr. Nearest Metro: Convention (12)

Messenger service
Allô-Courses. 8 Rue Blanche. Tel: 42.81.44.44
For motor-cycle/moped delivery service in Paris and outskirts.

Radio taxis
Tel: 42.03.99.99 or 47.39.33.33

They will ask for your address, the number of the arrondissement, and where you are going, but nothing else other than an approximate time of arrival. The taxi will appear as promised, but won't necessarily hang around if there is nowhere to park (other than at an hotel), so you will need to be ready and waiting or someone else will take it.

Telegrams
In English. Tel: 36.55

Telephones
Tourist events in English. Tel: 47.20.88.98
Speaking clock. Tel: 36.99
Paris weather. Tel: 45.55.95.90

RESTAURANTS

Restaurant	Address	Arr.
Chez Albert	122 Avenue du Maine	14
Allard	41 Rue St-André-des-Arts	6
Ambassade d'Auvergne	22 Rue du Grenier-St-Lazare	3
L'Ambroisie	65 Quai de la Tournelle	5
L'Ami Louis	32 Rue du Vertbois	3
Chez les Anges	54 Boulevard Latour-Maubourg	7
Annexe du Quai	3 Rue Surcouf	7
L'Aquitaine	54 Rue de Danzig	15
Les Armes de Bretagne	108 Avenue du Maine	14
Atelier Maître-Albert	1 Rue Maître-Albert	5
Auberge des Deux Signes	46 Rue Galande	5
Auberge Pyrénées Cévennes	106 Rue de la Folie-Méricourt	11
Aux Becs Fins	44 Boulevard de Ménilmontant	20
Benoit	20 Rue St-Martin	4
Beauvilliers	52 Rue Lamarck	18
Au Boeuf Couronné	188 Avenue Jean Jaurès	19
Bofinger	5 Rue de la Bastille	4
Brasserie Flo	6 Cour des Petites-Ecuries	10
La Boutique à Sandwiches	12 Rue du Colisée	8
Aux Charpentiers	10 Rue Mabillon	6
Clodenis	57 Rue Caulaincourt	18
La Closerie des Lilas	171 Boulevard du Montparnasse	6
Au Cochon d'Or	192 Avenue Jean Jaurès	19
Le Congrès	80 Avenue de la Grande-Armée	17
La Coquille	6 Rue Débarcadère	17
Le Coupe-Chou	11 Rue Lanneau	5
Dagorno	190 Avenue Jean Jaurès	19
Dodin-Bouffant	25–27 Rue Frédéric-Sauton	5
Escargot Montorgueil	38 Rue Montorgueil	1
Au Feu Follet	5 Rue Raymond-Losserand	14
La Ferme de la Villette	184 Avenue Jean Jaurès	19
La Ferme Saint-Simon	6 Rue Saint-Simon	7
Chez Frézet	181 Rue Ordener	18
La Gauloise	59 Avenue de La Motte-Picquet	15
Chez Gorisse	84 Rue Nollet	17
Le Grand Café	4 Boulevard des Capucines	9
La Grosse Tartine	91 Boulevard Gouvion-St-Cyr	17
Guy Savoy	28 Rue Duret	16
Le Jardin de la Paresse	Parc de Montsouris	14
Julien	16 Rue du Faubourg-St-Denis	10
Jules Verne	Eiffel Tower	7
Le Lord Gourmand	9 Rue Lord Byron	8
Marie-Louise	52 Rue Championnet	18
Mère Catherine	6 Place du Tertre	18

RESTAURANTS

Restaurant	Address	Arr.
Chez la Mère Michel	5 Rue Rennequin	17
Chez Michel	10 Rue de Belzunce	10
Michel Rostang	20 Rue Rennequin	17
Moissonnier	28 Rue des Fossés-St-Bernard	5
Morot-Gaudry	8 Rue de la Cavalerie	15
Le Morvan	22 Rue Chaligny	12
Le Paillon	4 Cour des Petites-Ecuries	10
Le Pain et Le Vin	1 Rue d'Armaille	17
Paul Chêne	123 Rue Lauriston	16
Chez Pauline	5 Rue Villedo	1
Le Pavillon du Lac	Parc des Buttes-Chaumont	19
Les Pavés de Tiquetonne	17 Rue Tiquetonne	2
La Petite Auberge	38 Rue Laugier	17
Le Petit Coin de la Bourse	16 Rue Feydeau	2
Le Petit Marguery	9 Boulevard de Port-Royal	13
Aux Petits Pères	8 Rue Notre-Dame-des-Victoires	2
Le Petit Pré	1 Rue Bellevue	19
Au Petit Riche	25 Rue le Peletier	9
Le Petit Zinc	25 Rue de Buci	6
Au Pied de Cochon	6 Rue Coquillière	1
Pierre Traiteur	10 Rue de Richelieu	1
Pierre Vedel	19 Rue Duranton	15
La Poularde Landaise	4 Rue St-Philippe-de-Roule	8
Le Procope	13 Rue l'Ancienne-Comédie	6
Au Quai des Ormes	72 Quai de l'Hôtel-de-Ville	4
Au Quai d'Orsay	49 Quai d'Orsay	7
Le Récamier	4 Rue Récamier	7
Relais de la Butte	12 Rue Ravignon	18
Relais des Pyrénées	1 Rue du Jourdain	19
Le Repaire de Cartouche	8 Boulevard des Filles-du-Calvaire	11
Sancerre	22 Avenue Rapp	8
Savy	23 Rue Bayard	8
A Sousceyrac	35 Rue Faidherbe	11
Taillevant	15 Rue Lamennais	8
Terminus Nord	23 Rue Dunkerque	10
Les Trois Portes	65 Rue La Fayette	9
Au Trou Gascon	40 Rue Taine	12
Ty-Coz	35 Rue St-Georges	9
Ty-Coz	333 Rue de Vaugirard	9
Le Train Bleu	Gare de Lyon	12
Le Vaudeville	29 Rue Vivienne	2
Chez la Vieille	37 Rue de l'Arbre-Sec	1
Les Vieux Métiers de France	13 Boulevard Auguste Blanqui	13
Le Wepler	14 Place Clichy	18

INDEX